JOSEPH BRONSON

THROUGH
THE GREEN

Golf Shots, Spots and Stories
Inspirations and Aspirations

**outskirts
press**

Outskirts Press, Inc.
http://www.outskirtspress.com

Paperback ISBN: 978-1-4787-9837-8
Hardback ISBN: 978-1-4787-9588-9

Library of Congress Control Number: 2018904855

Outskirts Press and the "OP" logo are trademarks belonging to Outskirts Press, Inc.

PRINTED IN THE UNITED STATES OF AMERICA

*This book is dedicated to my wife, Linda,
who gave me the freedom to have the time
to complete this work in fifteen months.*

*I would also like to acknowledge the contribution of
Michael Wishart, an accomplished senior amateur golfer
who has competed on the California Senior Amateur Tour.
Mike gave me some interesting ideas and insights that moti-
vated the fictional short story at the end of the book.*

PREFACE

When I completed and published the first book, *Golf Chronicles*, I thought I would be finished with writing about golf. *Chronicles* was written from an amateur's perspective without the expertise of instruction from professionals or expertise from the golf-writing media or even The Golf Channel. Now I have a web site with a blog that motivates me to write about golf in a way that you will never find in a newspaper. The book resonated with readers who really liked the format of the work as a series of vignettes and experiences of playing the game. There were a number of experiences and situations that were not covered in *Chronicles*, so I thought they must be covered. A golf book about difficult and enjoyable golf holes cannot exclude Bandon Dunes, so a complete chapter is devoted to this magical place. Through the Green will follow some of the similar format of the first book with another set of hardest holes, enjoyable holes, and international experiences. In this work, we will cover additional current insights of the state of the game, including media coverage and the latest developments in golf architecture. The big difference between *Golf Chronicles* and *Through the Green* is that a fictional short story has been inserted at the end of the book. The concept for doing a short story is to entertain the reader with a different concept of combining storytelling with a piece of fiction. The story is a fictional account of an amateur golfer who is attempting to climb to the highest levels of competitive amateur golf to a national championship.

My wife Linda continues to support me in my golfing habit and now has the additional responsibilities of keeping track of book sales and helping me with marketing materials, especially technology stuff on the computer.

Brian Shirley spent the 2017 Thanksgiving holiday with us in the US after a long hiatus in his new career as a grower and purveyor of British wine in his new digs in Somerset, England. At age seventy-five, he still has a golf swing to die for.

My son Ian continues to play well when he plays, which isn't often. He is into yoga, hiking, and other endeavors, and our golf together is limited to my birthday, Father's Day, Thanksgiving, and the Christmas holidays. He became a father on July 19, 2017 as Adrian Joseph Bronson entered this world. Adrian's golf clubs are on order. I beat Ian on my birthday, but I didn't brag about it. I just gave Linda the thumbs-up sign as we entered the house. Ian has decided to change the nature of scoring in golf and now keeps track of "whining" and bad language on his scorecard. Fortunately, I am not winning or leading in these categories, and my goal is not to score any points at all for these outbursts. Ian would recount a different story on this subject.

Meredith's clubs continue to gather dust in the closet and she continues to pursue her passion in swimming at the Master's Level. She got married in August 2016, so I am now determined to get her husband, James, into the game. I've already bought him some golf lessons. We had a golf outing for their wedding with seventeen participants.

TABLE OF CONTENTS

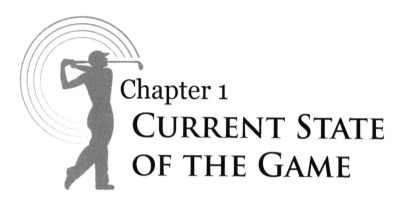

Chapter 1
CURRENT STATE
OF THE GAME

The game of golf continues to face significant issues despite favorable US economic conditions. A big problem is the inversion of the fee structure for the private golf club in the United States. It used to be a major investment for a family to place a substantial fee to enter the club and obtain an equity position in the club. Monthly dues and meals costs were very affordable and reasonable, so once the fee was paid, there were no issues for the family budget to be able to cover the monthly cost of dues and meals. Clubs use the monthly dues to cover the costs of maintaining the golf course and the facilities to the standard that persuaded the member/investor to join that particular club. Other significant matters for the family budget were the cost of education, especially private education, and the costs of housing. The cost of housing has now skyrocketed to the point where in some instances; the mortgage payment might be as much as 50% of the total family budget. These costs accelerated far faster than inflation and now the monthly dues for the country club have also tripled (for a private club on the West Coast over a fifteen-year period). The dues revenue from the member hardly covers the cost of maintaining the golf course and the facility, which requires the club to seek tournament play to generate revenue.

It's a vicious cycle to balance the budgets of the private country club, and in many cases, private country clubs have had to change their business model to survive. A new popular alternative is for the golf club to become a semi-private club, which means opening tee times to the public after a certain time to generate additional revenue and maintain the dues structure for the private members. It's not an easy model to execute, but it is a trend as marginal private clubs struggle to survive financially. In addition, there is a cultural side to how society views golf. The millennial generation now makes up the majority of the workforce. This is a generation that was raised with iPhones, iPads, and video games, which doesn't participate a great deal in golf. Of course, this is a generalization, but I think its fair to say that this is a group that lives with the smartphone and is looking for instant gratification. The group is disrupting traditional methods of shopping, retailing, and even education. Playing golf takes time and patience, and it's pretty difficult. Golf is now being played on game simulation technology, which is akin to a night at the bowling lane. Millennials don't want to spend the 4-5 hours that it takes to play a round. The video game provides instant gratification and scoring.

One significant positive development for the game is the return of Tiger Woods to the game. Tiger's return is for real this time, as he has overcome his physical ailments, which have plagued him the last few years. He has been competitive in all of his PGA Tour appearances and was actually considered to be a favorite at the 2018 Masters. TV ratings for tournaments where he has made the cut are terrific as once again, he is drawing the casual golf fan to fan enthusiast. Tiger's return is great for the game, and his future will be determined by his ability to overcome the mental part of the game in competition against younger players who are no longer intimidated by his presence.

Chapter 2
PEBBLE BEACH

In my travels around the world, when talking about golf and golf courses, people generally salivate when I begin to describe my residence in the 17 Mile Drive within Pebble Beach. I certainly take for granted my good fortune of having a residence there. Access to six of the country's top 100 golf courses within a five-mile area is certainly a wonderful benefit. There are many stories and books about Pebble Beach but in this work, I have decided to give the reader a significant insight into playing the golf course in a detailed hole-by-hole description. There are many people who tell me that it is their lifelong ambition to play the course, and this is written here for all of those golfers who have never played the course, maybe played it once, or have simply played the course on their computer in any of the myriad available golf web-based games.

OVERVIEW

The Pebble Beach course can be characterized as a wonderful walk by the sea with wonderful inland holes as well. Views of the Pacific Ocean begin at the third hole and continue through the 10th hole. You head to the clubhouse with two inland holes, 11 and 12, and then views of the Pacific return on 13, 14 heading a bit inland toward the 15th and 16th with a spectacular finish at the last two holes. Both professionals and amateurs alike would say that you have to score early on this course. The first seven holes of the course (with the possible exception of the 6th hole) present birdie opportunities to professionals and amateurs.

HOLE 1-PAR 4-377 YARDS

The first hole is pretty straightforward, but the experience of your first hole at Pebble Beach can be intimidating. The first hole adjoins the pro shop and there is likely to be a number of onlookers headed to the retail outlets of Pebble Beach or those patrons having breakfast at the Gallery Restaurant, which overlooks the first hole. If you've never played the course before and you're a bit squeamish about the first tee shot, you'll be trying to pay some attention to what's in front of you.

The first hole is a short par 4, but the tee shot has to be carved into the middle of the fairway or at the left side of the fairway. There are a bunch of fir trees to the right side of the fairway, and any tee shot hit to the right will punish the player. There will be no shot to the green, and the only option is to take the medicine and chip the ball out to the middle of the fairway or try to advance it for a 50-75-yard pitch shot. Conversely, if the tee shot is a bit too far to the left, even if it's in the fairway, the second shot will be difficult, as there is a series of overhanging trees on the left which will require more precision that you would have wanted from hitting the ball in the fairway. Professionals and low-handicap players may generally hit 3 woods off the tee for this hole to get into the proper position for the approach shot.

Two large bunkers border the putting green, which can be penal depending on the lie. The bunkers can also be intimidating to the 30-50-yard pitch shot, as any type of mishit will produce a very negative result.

The first green is on the small side and generally requires a very precise iron shot to get close to the pin, which is usually in the middle of the green. The green tends to have breaks toward the ocean, but the pace of this green seems to have the ball accelerate as it approaches this middle-pin position. In general, it is recommended that the ball be kept below the hole at Pebble Beach. I find another discriminating feature on this hole is that any errant shots right or left will be more penal to the player than on most holes. The left side of the hole is marked by a thicket of trees and long grasses that are impossible to get out of.

2ND HOLE-PAR 5, 460 YARDS

If you have survived the nerves of completing the first hole at Pebble, the second hole is certainly not easy but very playable without much difficulty. It's almost telling you, "You can calm down now and start playing golf." The hole is a straightaway generous fairway with bunkers on the right and the left and could catch an errant tee shot. There is a risk/reward element to this hole, as there is a gully about 75 yards from the green that has to be covered. For most amateurs, it will be a 3-shot hole to the green. Even if the tee shot is crushed about 270-280 yards, the fairway to green funnels in a bit. Any shot that intends to try to get home in 2 will require a wood or long iron to cross the gully. If you hit the drive 250 yards into the fairway, you will need almost 200 yards to carry the gully which is a low percentage shot for the amateur. The best way to play the hole is to hit the second shot from the fairway to about 100 yards (25 yards from the gully) and keep the ball in the middle of the fairway. There are trees that mark each side of the gully and can come into play if you're in the wrong position. Two bunkers guard each side of the green and will catch many errant fairway iron shots. The green is a tricky one to putt, as it usually faster than it appears, especially around the pin position. This is definitely a birdie hole for the professional and low-handicap player who can cross the gully in 2 shots to try and get an eagle putt. As a result, I would imagine that this hole is one of the easiest holes on tour.

The hole is a confidence-builder for the amateur who can

get the tee shot into the fairway, and the opportunity to recover from a poor shot is possible on this hole.

3rd Hole, par 4, 374 yards

The third hole used to be easier than it is now. New tees were installed about seven years ago, which added length to the hole. The hole is a dogleg to the left, requiring a tee shot in the middle of the fairway or slightly to the right. There are 3 bunkers in the middle of the fairway designed to catch the tee shot that is hit through the fairway. These bunkers are "par killers" for the amateur. Any tee shot hit too far right on the fairway will lengthen the hole considerably to 160-170 yards. There is a risk/reward tee shot for the player who can hit the ball long and draw the ball around the dogleg. Professionals can do this and end up with wedge shots or less to the green. The approach shot to this green presents some potentially interesting challenges. From the fairway, the hole slants from right to left, with a very penal bunker on the right side of the green. Most lies in this bunker will be downhill, which most of us find to be the most difficult bunker shots. Any shot hit through this green will result in a big number—definitely a no-no. Any approach shot missed to the right of this hole will face a very difficult chip shot and virtually impossible to stop on the green. From the fairway, my strategy is to drop down a club and have the ball run up to the pin instead of going pin-seeking with a lofted club. Tiger Woods made a 7 on this hole in his US Open march in 2000, which was one of the few blemishes on his card for the week.

The hole sits in a great location for spectators for tournament viewing, as the 3rd green adjoins the 17th tee and is 50 yards from the 4th tee. Another lesser-known fact is that a cypress tree that was situated on the left side of the 3rd fairway about 175 yards out was removed from that site to replace the dead cypress on the 18th hole that guards the green. I believe it was 3 years that the 18th had gone without a cypress tree, since it is very difficult for such transplants to work. I had the good fortune to be playing with Arnold Palmer at Pebble, the first day that the tree was liberated from its transplant wires and took its place on 18.

4TH HOLE, PAR 4, 307 YARDS

A very interesting hole that is full of risk/reward. An overview of the hole is as follows:

- There is a huge bunker that crosses the fairway and must be carried between 175-190 yards.
- There are bunkers on the left past the huge bunker that may catch a tee shot that's hit on the left side.
- There is not much room on the right side, either, as this is your first view of the Pacific Ocean. Any tee shot hit to the right with any kind of "slice" spin will end up in the Pacific.
- The tiny green is completely surrounded by bunkers on all sides.
- The green is at a point at the top of the rocks overlooking the Pacific. A great view, but don't go over the

green, or else the ball will either be lost to the rocks below or in the bunker.

So, how does one play this hole? The professional decides rather quickly if he wants to drive the tee shot to the green. Most, if not all, of today's professionals have the capability to drive the green. However, it's a very risky play, in my view, since the green is so small. Professionals are likely to put the ball in one of the bunkers surrounding the green if they miss it. It won't be easy getting up and down out of these bunkers, but this strategy creates the birdie opportunity. Some professionals will choose to drive the ball to a spot that they like, where they can spin the ball to the pin position for their birdie opportunity.

For the amateur, it's a different situation. The tee shot must carry the huge bunker requiring a high shot, such as a hybrid or utility club, to have a 100-110 yard shot into the green. Putting downhill on this green is to be avoided, so approach shots must be below the hole to give the amateur a birdie opportunity. The 4th is the beginning of spectacular ocean views that continue from here to the 11th tee box. The Pebble Beach-Beach Club adjoins the 4th hole with its facilities and boat dock in full view of the hole.

5TH HOLE—PAR 3, 142 YARDS

The 5th hole is actually the newest hole to grace the Pebble Beach Golf Links. It's about 20 years old now. The old 5th hole was an afterthought and clearly an embarrassment to this wonderful golf course. The old 5th moved slightly inland and played to about 165 yards uphill. It was completely non-descript compared to the rest of the golf course, and something needed to be done. It was desirable to bring another hole to the seaside. There was a home on the existing site of the new 5th, so that home had to be purchased and demolished. There were other homes and land needed to provide the proper venue for a newly designed golf hole. The new 5th was open for play in 1998 and is an immediate treasure with wonderful views of Stillwater Cover and the Pacific Ocean. The new par 3 plays a comfortable 150 yards for the amateur gold tees and 190 yards from the back tees. It's not an easy hole for the professional to make birdie here, as the tee shot demands accuracy. The green is lengthy, but not much in width, and slopes from right to left. Shots executed to the left of the green will move right into those pin positions. For the amateur, birdie is possible due to comfortable length of the hole depending on the wind-a 7 or 8 iron is enough. There is a bunker guarding the green to the right and one in the back of the green, but they really shouldn't come into play for a well-struck shot. Trouble is possible for shots hit through the green, as the ball will land in rough that is usually "spinachy" and can be wet. Recovery pitch shots are straight down hill and treacherous, so I believe this is the only way to get into difficulty on this hole. The hole is nestled nicely into Stillwater Cove, providing some wonderful views of the coastline.

6TH HOLE, PAR 5, 506 YARDS

This is a potential birdie hole for the professional, but it presents a pretty significant challenge for the amateur. It is certainly the most difficult of the first seven holes on the course. I claim these holes are all birdie potential holes for the professional. This is the part of the golf course that can be attacked by the professional. The tee shot isn't easy, but it has to be long, or else the second shot is almost impossible.

AN OVERVIEW:

- Tee box is slightly uphill, giving you a downhill tee shot, which will add yardage to the tee shot providing that the wind is cooperative.

- There are 3 menacing bunkers on the left side of the fairway. Landing in one of these bunkers will add a stroke to both professional and amateur alike.

- The fairway is wide and quite generous, but the position in the fairway is very important to hitting the next shot.

- The fairway ends at about 310 yards facing a "wall" of rough that has to be carried to get to the upper tier of the hole where the green is. During the 2000 US Open, Tiger Woods mystified the crowd with a tee shot of over 300 yards to the base of the wall, leaving him with an iron shot to the green for an eagle attempt. I can't remember seeing any professional driving it that far with that type of accuracy. Clearly Woods was the height of his powers, and eventually won the event by over 10 strokes over his nearest competitor.

It is imperative to get the second shot over this "wall" to get an approach shot to the green for birdie. If the tee shot is not long enough, the best option is to lay up to the wall for another go, or hit the ball way left to the top of the hill to avoid landing the ball in the rough on the wall. Any shot required from the rough on the wall is essentially a wasted shot and can lead to big numbers on this hole. The second shot is essentially "blind," so you have to set a strategy that will enable par or at least bogey, depending on the situation. If the tee shot is hit to the right on the fairway, the carry over the wall for the next shot is even more difficult, since there is no room on the right side of the top tier of the hole (it will be in the ocean). I wouldn't say that this is a birdie hole for the amateur, but par is a distinct possibly if the second shot is executed correctly.

7ᵀᴴ HOLE-PAR 3, 107 YARDS

The venerable 7th hole has graced many a golf publication, and it is probably the most-photographed hole in all of golf. I used my own photograph of the hole myself for *Golf Chronicles*. It's not hard to describe, since it's been viewed and played by millions of golf fans. The hole is actually "too easy," which is what makes it difficult. You approach the 7th with birdie on your mind, and the hole actually plays in your mind. It would be embarrassing to miss the green or not make par. One of the worst things a golfer can do is to plot the score he's going to make on a hole that hasn't been played yet. Club selection is critical—pitching wedge, sand wedge (52 or 56 degrees) is usually the club. I hit my gap wedge (52 degrees) on this hole if there is no wind.

There have been times when this hole is into the wind, and I once played a round with Arnold Palmer where we both hit 4 irons into this hole with a 40-mph wind in our face. It takes a lot of courage to take a full swing with a 4 iron on a 107-yard hole and get that ball into the wind, which will force it down, onto the green. If you try to hit a half shot, the shot will be missed and sent down below to the Pacific Ocean. You can be long sometimes on this green, but it's a razor-thin margin to those rocks down below. Perhaps this is one of the best views on the face of the earth, when the sun is shining.

8ᵀᴴ HOLE, PAR 4, 400 YARDS

The 8th hole is the beginning of a series of very difficult holes, particularly for the amateur player. Two sets of tees are used here. The lower tees present an uphill tee shot that can travel no more than 240 yards to the gorge that has to be crossed to get to the green below. So, you drive the ball up into the fairway and then down to the green below.

From the lower tees, a stone marker gives you the direction to approach the fairway. The left side is better than the right side, but the key is length of the tee shot. You want to get as close to that gorge as possible without going into it. This tee shot will give you 175-180 yards to one of the trickiest greens on the golf course. Tee shots that are in the fairway but too far from the gorge have difficult decisions to make. The best choice is to pick a club that can carry the gorge and leave you with a 30-50- yard pitch shot into the green. An aggressive play hoping for a miracle, or a shot that you hit well one out of ten times, is not called for here. Tom Kite almost lost the 1992 US Open when his iron shot failed to carry the gorge and miraculously got stuck in the rough guarding the green. If the rough had been normal and not USGA brutal rough, there would have been nothing to stop the ball careening into the beach below. I find the putting surface on this green diabolical—you just have to be below the hole. Not many putts are holed on this green by either professional or amateur.

9ᵀᴴ HOLE, PAR 4, 460 YARDS

This hole is difficult for both professional and amateur alike. The length of the hole and the potential for windy conditions make this hole very difficult to reach in regulation for the professional. The amateur that hits the ball with great length will still have the same difficulty as the professional. The 9ᵗʰ has a generous fairway for the tee shot with a fairway bunker about 260 yards on the left side that cannot be reached if the wind is blowing. The second shot for the amateur is to keep the ball in the fairway as the fairway begins to narrow from the tee shot with the Pacific and beach to the right side of the hole. Prevailing wind is left to right, taking a high shot and moving it toward the Pacific. The best play is to keep the ball in the fairway and get it to a range of 75-100 yards where a lofted shot can be used to get close to the pin. If the ball is closer in, say 40-50 yards, I would recommend keeping the ball out of the air through a bump-and-run shot. The green is reasonably sized, but all putts will break toward the ocean quite severely. A menacing bunker guards the left side of the green and must be avoided, as it is so deep that extricating the ball from that bunker will not be easy, and at a minimum, will be difficult to get close to the hole. This is one of the most difficult holes on the PGA Tour and plays usually to a tournament score of 4.3 or higher.

10ᵀᴴ HOLE, PAR 4, 446 YARDS

The 10th is the last hole on the Pacific coast as you begin to head inland. It is another beast, as the third tough hole in a row. It is very similar to the 9th hole, with additional bunkers in the fairway, and plays very long into a prevailing wind that is generally against the player. The strategy for playing the hole is the same as the 9th, but the 10th hole has more challenges on the left side, with serious contouring of the hole toward the ocean, and a number of bunkers on the left side. The length of the hole brings all of these challenges into play as the fairway narrows with the Pacific on the right side to catch any errant shot. The prevailing wind is the same as the 9th, as these two holes are pure links golf holes. Positioning on the fairway is an absolute to try to get close enough to make par. This is yet another hole that makes the PGA toughest list with an average score of 4.3.

11TH HOLE, PAR 4, 373 YARDS

The 11th is the beginning of the way home from the grueling passage of 8 through 10, but that doesn't mean it gets any easier. The 11th has a generous fairway that is below the hole, so the drive is blind but directionally understandable. The only mistake that can be made here would be to push the tee shot to the right. There is nothing good on the right of this hole, so it just has to be avoided at any cost. The key shot on the hole is the approach shot to the green. The green is horizontal in shape and not very deep, so it's easy to either fly the green or dump the shot into the front bunker. This green is one of the most treacherous holes to putt on the entire golf course. The pin is usually placed in the middle of the green, and there are subtle breaks throughout; it putts much faster than it appears. I find short putts on this hole diabolical, as there are subtle breaks near the hole. The green is the reason why this par 4 is not a birdie hole. Anything hit over the green will have a delicate pitch back to the pin, as the speed of the green is faster than one might think. The rough on this hole is usually higher than some of the other holes, increasing the difficulty of the approach to the pin.

12TH HOLE, PAR 3, 190 YARDS

This hole is a strong par 3 because of its bunkering. There are bunkers guarding the green on all sides of the hole. The hole usually plays into a prevailing wind that pushes the tee shot from left to right. Due to the bunkering on the hole, the amateur has no choice but to hit a very high shot that will carry the bunkers and keep the ball on the green. This green is very large but relatively straightforward. Any shot on the green should enable a 2-putt par. If you miss the green and all the bunkers, there's a reasonable chance of converting a par from the rough that is on all sides of the green. The professional should have no difficulty with this hole and can hit a 7 or 8 iron to the hole to this very large green. There aren't a lot of birdies on this hole and the hole also ranks as one of the toughest Par 3's on the PGA Tour with an average score of 3.3.

13TH HOLE, 390 YARDS, PAR 4

After completing the 12th, you are ready to re-embrace the sea as you come home. The 13th fairway is a beautiful hole that adjoins the 9th in true links style. There is a bunker in the middle of the fairway that continues up the left side of the hole and will catch many amateur tee shots. Prevailing wind is usually against the player, and the hole gently moves uphill. There are bunkers on the right side that won't catch many amateur shots but can receive professional shots, as those bunkers start at about the 240-yard mark and continue to at least 270. The approach shot to this green is critical, as the green severely slopes from the right to the ocean side. Approach shots must be pin high or a little farther and to the right, so that the ball will trickle down to the left and approach the hole. The ball will continue to move to that hole and sometimes will pick up speed, turning a good approach shot and birdie opportunity into a difficult opportunity for par. The first time that someone plays this hole, it is very difficult for them to judge how far to the right of the pin is required. Anything hit short or to the left of the pin will roll off the green and leave a very challenging pitch shot. This is a hole that looks easy but is anything but easy. Your approach shot must be at least 40 feet to the right of the pin, which is usually placed on the left side of the hole. A well-executed shot to the green will release to the hole, which will really surprise the player who is playing the course for the first time.

14ᵀᴴ HOLE, PAR 5, 560 YARDS

The 14th hole is one of the most difficult holes on the PGA Tour. When I first started playing Pebble many years ago, I thought that this was a hole that I should par every time. I would hit a tee shot, a 3 wood and an 8 or 9 iron into the green, 2-putt and make my par. Well, the hole was redesigned a little and the changes have now made par an outstanding score for me. The hole was lengthened by some 30 yards, which has a significant impact on the 3rd shot into the green. This is a 3-shot hole for both professional and amateur. It's a 4-shot hole for the high-handicapper. The fairway is very generous and one of the widest and most accessible on the course. You simply have to pound the ball out there some 250 yards, if you want to have an opportunity to make par. The second shot simply has to be struck well and far to give you a chance to have a potential approach to the green. The biggest change to this hole was the contouring of the green and the rough surrounding the hole. An enormous bunker that you definitely want to avoid guards the hole. The rough around the green has been mown down so it now has a type of "Pinehurst No. 2" effect where all missed shots will roll to the bottom of a type of receiving area for errant approach shots. The pitch shot back to a green where the pin position is crowned is very difficult, and many professionals end up making bogey on this hole. This hole was the most difficult in the US Open, where the average score for the entire field was over par.

The length of the hole creates a real challenge for the amateur. The last time I played the hole, I hit a poor short tee shot and then belted a 3 wood 230 yards just inside the out-of-bounds marker on the left side. It was a terrible place to be, but I was inside the out-of-bounds marker and had a 155 yard shot to the hole. I didn't have much to lose, so I chose a 6 iron and flushed it just over the bunker to about 10 feet from the hole. I had a birdie putt, which I missed, but it was a very improbable par on this tough hole.

15TH HOLE, PAR 4, 377 YARDS

This is a beautifully designed hole as you start to make your way home. The hole is parallel to the 17-mile drive toward the main gate of the Pebble Beach Lodge, and it's a great spectator location for viewing the professionals. The tee shot has to clear trees, which flank the left and right side of the entrance to the fairway. The trees are like goal posts on a football field, introducing you to the generous fairway that is slightly downhill. A tee shot hit to the right will still result in a potential shot to the green, whereas a tee shot hit to the left will potentially produce no option to the green. The look of the hole is so inviting that you feel that you just have to make par. Sometimes club selection is difficult, because there is usually at least a wisp of wind that you really can't feel from the fairway. Bunkers that guard the green really shouldn't be in play, since there is plenty of room to get on the green. The green seems large for this type of par 4, and putting presents some challenges, as there are a number of insidious breaks that are very tough to read. I've seen a number of 3- putt bogeys from professionals here, which is very frustrating for the professional who probably believes that this is a birdie hole. It simply is not.

16ᵀᴴ HOLE, PAR 4, 376 YARDS

The 16th has one of the widest fairways on the golf course. There is a fairway bunker about 200 yards from the tee, which should not come into play for amateurs and professionals alike. The wide fairway shrinks rapidly for the approach shot into the green. Trouble starts to lurk in many places. Any tee shot hit to the right side of the fairway will require a very good shot to the green—for amateurs, it's a low- percentage shot but has to be attempted. The shot will have to cover the trees and a huge bunker that covers the entire fairway about 50 yards from the green. Any tee shot hit to the left side of the fairway will give you an open shot to the green, but the distance will be longer from that position. My son, Ian, hit a poor tee shot down the left side of the fairway and had over 200 yards to the green. Of course, he proceeded to take out his driver and holed the shot for an Eagle 2—a once in a lifetime achievement! The green also has a series of subtle breaks, and many of the putts are double breakers to the hole, especially if the pin is on the right side of the green.

17ᵀᴴ HOLE, PAR 3—175 YARDS

In my opinion, this hole is one of the greatest par-3 holes in the world and the site of many exciting professional tour events. The most notable memory for me is Tom Watson's chip in from the thick rough on the left side of the hole for birdie in the last round (71ˢᵗ hole) of the 1982 United States Open (the shot heard round the world).

On a sunny day on the Monterey Peninsula, it might be the most beautiful hole in the world. The hole is shaped by the Pebble Beach Club facility on the left, moving up to Stillwater Cove. The green is long vertically, maybe 35 yards, but skinny on the horizontal side. The hole is completely protected by bunkers, which are always in play and pretty difficult to get the ball close to the pin, as there isn't a lot of green to work with from any position in these bunkers.

The USGA has made this hole very difficult for the professional in the US Opens that have been played here since the 2000 US Open. The tee has been pushed back to a yardage approaching 200 yards. The hole was never designed to be played at this distance, given the dimensions of the green. The results of this tee position resulted in the 17th as the second-most-difficult hole on the course, with a field average score over par.

For the daily fee player at Pebble, the hole plays 165-170 yards. Wind makes club selection very interesting, as the back pin placement causes the hole to play at least 190 yards. Depending on skill level—it's a 7 iron or a 5 wood with potentially very unpredictable results. At the AT&T Pro-AM, contestants continually missed the green to the right of the hole, as wind that could not be felt on the tee pushed tee shots to the right, resulting in a number of bogeys or worse. The professionals in the event often under-clubbed as well, despite their significant skills.

18ᵀᴴ HOLE—PAR 5, 532 YARDS

The venerable signature hole on the Pebble Beach Golf links is beautiful conclusion and one of the most scenic holes on the planet. It is a 3-shot hole for professional and amateur alike. The Pacific Ocean is the view on the left side of the hole all the way to the green. The fairway is generous for the tee shot, with a large cypress tree right in the middle of the fairway about 300 yards from the tee box. Some players approach the tee shot trying to avoid those trees for their second shot and flirt with the ocean. Many amateur tee shots that choose this route end up on the rocks and ocean below. Most players choose the center or right side of the fairway leaving a second shot that must go around the tree in the fairway where a shot to the green is possible. A seawall with a bunker that extends about 75 yards all the way to the green protects the left side of the fairway to the green. A second shot to the left might catch this bunker. The green is protected on the right by a huge cypress tree and another bunker, which must be covered to get the ball on the green. The original cypress tree died on this hole, and for a few years, there was no tree to guard the green. Efforts to find a replacement were difficult, as the challenge to have a cypress tree of the same height had to be transplanted. After a few years, a cypress tree that bordered the 3rd hole that wasn't even in play was transplanted to the site on the 18th successfully. I had the good fortune of playing the hole with Arnold Palmer for the first time with the newly transplanted tree. The green has a number of subtle breaks at the various pin positions. It's a great experience walking up the 18th hole with the lodge in view on the right side of the hole. Usually there is a gallery of Pebble Beach guests looking on and taking in the beautiful scenery and watching the playing public player trying to do their best on this beautiful hole.

As you hole the final putt, the exhilaration of playing one of the best courses ever begins to set in and you can't wait to take another shot at it.

Chapter 3
BANDON DUNES

There are many books written about Bandon Dunes, which I could not do justice to. These books detail how the course was formed, designed and all the details you could have ever wanted to know about this Mecca of Golf. This chapter relates to the experience that I believe the golfer will have and can relate to. I have been to Bandon several times and will never tire of going there, but I want to give the reader of this book the experience from the player/visitor's point of view.

Bandon Dunes is a difficult place to get to in North Bend, Oregon. You used to have to fly north to Portland and then get on another flight to North Bend. It was a long day and almost 7-8 hours of flying time. United Airlines now has a direct flight out of San Francisco directly to North Bend. As usual, United charges a hefty premium for this service in a regional jet that takes only about an hour and a half from San Francisco direct to North Bend. If you're staying at the resort, which I recommend highly, the resort will pick you up, so there is really no need for a rental car. Once you are on-property, you will want to stay put. The resort consists of a main lodge building where there are a few rooms. The rest of the lodging in the resort is a series of bungalows situated throughout the complex where you are picked up and transported wherever you need to go. Each bungalow typically has four bedrooms with private baths, a common living area with TV's and amenities that are very comfortable. You'll find yourself not using much of the common area, as you'll be exhausted from the golf and will welcome your bedroom. The main lodge building contains an area for lunch and a full dining room where you essentially eat every night. The food is terrific, and the wine list is superb. I get a little chuckle out of the fitness center in the main building; there is no time to use it, as you will consume all of your energy walking 18 holes every day. Some players will walk 36 holes, which I would find impossible. Next to the main building is the pro shop, club storage, and caddy shack. Bandon courses are walking courses for golf—you will walk the golf course every day with caddies. The caddies are knowledgeable and very experienced. The rest of the complex consists of a pub where you can brag about your great golf shots, settle up the day's bets, and generally fill the air with a lot of great stories. Outside the pub, a blazing fire is fueled nightly for those imbibing with cigars and their favorite scotch or Irish whiskey.

You come to Bandon to eat, sleep, and drink golf and literally nothing else, so any other expectations should be shelved.

There is a portion of the visiting legion of golfers who decide to roll into North Bend to a casino, which will probably lead to a hangover for the following day's first tee. Bandon Dunes is not Pebble Beach, Torrey Pines, or Pinehurst. It was not designed for luxury and guest amenities-it was designed for you to play golf and get enough good food and sustenance to keep playing for the time you are going to be there. This is the charm of Bandon—it is simple and not pretentious, it is comfortable but not luxurious—the goal is to get you on those golf courses and create the best golf experience you have ever had.

There are currently four fabulous 18-hole courses along with a 13-hole par-3 course and a sumptuous driving range with a pitch and putt layout for further practice. The courses are Bandon Dunes, Pacific Dunes, Bandon Trails, and Old MacDonald. Bandon, Pacific and Old MacDonald are links with spectacular ocean views on many of the holes. I believe that all the courses rate rank in the Top 100 of Golf Courses in the United States, and Pacific Dunes is currently ranked No. 1. There is no housing, no cart paths, essentially no carts, firm turf for running shots and large greens. All the courses are walking courses with caddies. There are a few golf carts to accommodate those players who can't walk the courses, but there are no cart paths to spoil the scenery and the ambience of the place.

Weather at Bandon can be dodgy. You have to bring the waterproof rain gear, rain gloves, woolen beanie, jackets and windbreakers and be prepared for anything. The weather adds to the mystique of the venue. In summer, you can tee off at Bandon Dunes in considerable fog and cold with absolutely no wind. By the time you have ended your round, the sun can be beating down on you and the winds begin to whip up and become a factor. On summer days, the day at Pacific Dunes or Bandon Dunes will have completely different conditions if you play in the morning or in the afternoon. In the morning, it will be on the cold side with little to no wind. In the afternoon, the sun is likely to be warm, but the winds can blow considerably to 20-25 miles per hour or harder. Links golf requires a lot of patience and concentration, as you will get some strange bounces from the fairways. Bandon's fairways are as perfect as Turnberry, Scotland with hard and fast turf. If you didn't know where you were, conditions are equivalent to playing any of the links courses in Scotland, England, or Ireland.

My favorite track at Bandon is Trails. Trails is not a links course but, in my view, seems to be a hybrid of a parkland layout with trees throughout the course combined with spectacular natural terrain that also has the look of a links course but is not a links course. I like Trails the best of all the courses because it's a course I can score on. For most of the round, the course meanders through the forest until you get to the 16th hole and prepare to come in. The wind usually is always present on the closing holes, and the 18th is a great closing hole and one of my favorites. Old MacDonald is a very hard course. It's difficult to explain, because the course is not inherently hard but the wind at Old MacDonald seems to blow hard all the time, throwing shots everywhere. Patience is required, and the greens are the size of the Old Course at St. Andrews. Four putting at Old MacDonald is equivalent to three-putting on most golf courses due to the size of the greens. Bandon Dunes seems to be the fairest and most interesting layout. It has a generous mixture of holes that require you hit almost every club in the bag. It is the original course that was first built, and it is usually the first course you play at Bandon Dunes.

BANDON TRAILS

Bandon Trails was designed by Bill Coore and Ben Crenshaw. Previously, Coore and Crenshaw had designed Sand Hills in Nebraska, which is a top 100 course. Bandon Trails is a tree-lined "forest course" in the coastal woodlands on the inland side of Back Ridge on the property. The idea was to build a course, unlike the other links courses, that would be tree-lined and not have the significant impact of wind on play. The interesting part of Trails is there is forest, meadow, dunes (with gorse) without the wind. Trails is truly an ambient stroll through the quiet of the trees, links-like turf, and large greens where the short game is very important to score. The course plays at 6,857 yards from the championship tees to a par of 71. I really like the par 5, 3rd hole that measures 549 yards. The hole has a very wide fairway, and you must maneuver around a number of well-placed bunkers to approach a very large green in regulation. I always choose the right side of the fairway, to avoid the bunkers setting up a long iron or hybrid club for the short 3rd approach shot to the green. The hole seems like it was easy to design, as it meanders through the forest. The par 3, fifth hole is only 133 yards, which is all carry over the gorse and guarded by menacing front bunkers. The hole looks harmless from the tee box, but you must hit the green with enough depth in order to have a good opportunity for birdie. If the ball takes off to the back of the hole, a three-putt or even four-putt may be in your future. As you continue to play on, you approach the 9th hole, and the environment seems to be getting even quieter as you are surrounded by forest with towering fir and spruce trees. The lake on the 11th hole to the right of the green is as still as glass. Bandon Trails is a course that I could play every day and never tire of it.

PACIFIC DUNES

Pacific is always rated in the top ten of public courses in the United States. It was the second course developed in the complex and designed by Tom Doak. Pacific starts out in a benign way and gets harder and harder as you progress. My sensation is that the start at Pacific is easier than Bandon Dunes, but the course gets tougher and tougher. The first hole at Pacific is a short par 4, which looks very easy, but the landing area for the tee shot is hidden and the green is very small with undulations throughout. Par on this hole is a very good score. The second hole offers an elevated tee, which provides a wonderful view of the course and the Pacific Ocean in the distance. The hole is a par 4, measuring 368 yards.

Fairway bunkers are well placed, as the player has to decide how to carry these bunkers and create an angle for the shot to the green. The green is pretty small, and a short iron that is too long may find the dunes at the rear of the green. You breathe a healthy sigh of relief as you move to the 3rd hole, a par 5 of 499 yards. The hole offers the widest fairway on the course and one of the widest fairways you will find anywhere. You are now proceeding to the ocean and three good shots can yield a birdie here.

The easy 3rd hole gives way to the treacherous 463-yard, par 4, 4th hole. The hole is breathtaking, bordering the ocean on the right side of the fairway. Any tee shot that fades or heads to the right could end up on the beach below, as there is no room for error here. The green is surrounded by gorse, weeds. and horrendous vegetation that will devour the golf ball that lands in it. The par 3, 5th hole is all carry of 180 yards to avoid all the sea grasses, weeds, and gorse that surround the green. There are no bunkers here by the green, which is immense (similar to the size of Old MacDonald's greens), where four-putting is a possibility. The 7th hole is a difficult 464 par 4, which requires three shots to the green for most players (including me). There are two fairways—uphill and downhill, with a hazard of gorse and brush in the middle of the fairway. Depending on how the wind is blowing, it's likely that you will play the tee shot from the downhill fairway due to the length of the hole. The second shot must carry the plateau of rough in the fairway to the uphill part of the fairway for an approach shot of 50-100 yards depending on the wind. The approach shot will have to be accurate and avoid flying the green, where you would have to deal with more dunes. The next two holes are easier and very beautiful, where you can get on in two and relax a little bit. The 10th and 11th holes are back-to-back par 3's. No. 10 is 206 yards with the ocean on the left. There isn't a lot of room for a long par 3 especially due to wind conditions. The carry across the environmental elements is over 170 yards and a straight shot towards the hole is required. A shot pulled to the left could end up in a watery grave or the beach below and the right side is full of heather and gorse that will make a pitch shot to the green extremely difficult. The 11th hole is only 148 yards, but it's a lot harder than No. 10. The hole is uphill all the way from tee to green and the prevailing wind is usually in your face or crossing off the ocean from left to right. Club selection is difficult as the hole actually plays at least 160 yards and any offline shots will be severely penalized. The hole can be frustrating, as the tricky wind seems to throw shots everywhere. After battling through these two par 3's, you can relax a bit as you arrive at the par 5, 12th hole of 529 yards due to its generous fairway. The ambience of this hole is calming for the player as three solid shots can produce a birdie opportunity. You're back in the "soup" on the par 4, 13th hole of 444 yards. The tee shot must carry the oceanic terrain in front of you and reminds me of the tee position for the drive on the 18th hole at Pebble Beach. The position of the tee shot is all-important since most players aren't going to hit this green in regulation. A tee shot to the right of the fairway will lengthen the hole considerably and make it difficult to get in a pitching position for the third shot to this green. The hole boasts a huge sand hill on the right of the fairway, so if you end up there, you will lose at least one shot. The land at the green on this hole, as this is the northernmost point on the course as you can hear the waves crashing against the rocks below.

Holes 14-17 present the player with a variety of different shots and they are the easiest and most playable on the back nine. The toughest hole on the course is the 18th, a par 5 of 591 yards. It's very challenging to reach this green in regulation.

Due to the wind, it will probably take four shots to get to this green. My opinion is that it's better to hit a pitch shot 80-100 yards for the 4th shot and increase your chances of making a putt for par rather than trying to reach the green from 170 yards with a four iron in your hand trying to avoid all the treacherous bunkering on both sides of the hole. The 18th is a culmination of all the difficult aspects of Pacific Dunes-wind, heather, gorse, bunkers are all in play. You simply have to try to get a shot close in to make that par at the end of this wonderful layout.

BANDON DUNES

Bandon Dunes is the first course that was built on the resort. It is a links layout that starts out a bit intimidating since the first hole is an uphill par 4 and a dogleg to the left. It's usually cold in the morning and you really don't know where you're going, so the tee shot has to be accurate in this fairway. The course meanders out to the sea, out into the wind, the dunes, the gorse, and all the rest of the elements. It's difficult to make a par on the first hole, primarily due to club selection, as the hole plays longer than the stated yardage due to the wind and uphill conditions. It's difficult for the caddie to give you the right stick, as it's the first hole that he's observing your play. The second hole is an uphill par 3 of 189 yards, which is yet another challenge of club selection due to the wind conditions. You begin to worry that you came a long way to enjoy yourself and this course, which is your first experience at Bandon, looks like it's going to be a grind.

Not to worry—you arrive at the 3rd tee, a par 5 of 543 yards, and now you know why you came here. The fairway is immense and dotted with bunkers that should be avoidable. There is a beautiful view of the Pacific Ocean from the tee box over the bluffs, and the hole simply invites you to stripe it into the fairway and make a certain par. After the 3rd, you proceed ever closer to the ocean. The par-4, 428 yard 5th hole is a spectacular hole. You tee off with the Pacific to your left and the tee shot has to land in the fairway and avoid the grass-tufted mounds that can come into play. Unlike Irish courses that sport these types of mounds, these mounds are functional markers that seem to act as beacons as to where to drive the tee ball. The second shot is a long iron to the green with a fairway that gets narrower as you approach it. The hole is surrounded by gorse, mounding, and nasty stuff that has to be avoided. This hole can be very difficult depending on the direction of the wind, but its design is very pleasing to the eye. After the wonderful experience on the 5th, you approach the 6th tee, a par 3 of 181 yards. This hole is right on the Pacific Ocean and it's so quiet that you have the feeling that you might be in Ireland or Scotland, not Oregon. After the 6th, the course turns inward and the first start toward the clubhouse. The 9th hole is a par 5 of 558 yards, which reminds me of the 10th hole of the Shore Course at the Monterey Peninsula Country Club in Pebble Beach, California. The tee shot should be as left as possible to attempt to chop off the distance of the hole (missing it will be perilous). The hole demands three good shots to the green so a birdie or a par is possible here.

Completing the turn on the front 9, the course again heads back out to the sea starting on the par-4, 362 yard 10th hole. This hole is relatively straightforward, as it winds a bit to the right, guarded by a giant bunker. The 11th hole is difficult, caused mostly by wind as you approach the ocean for the first time on the back nine. The prevailing wind is usually off the ocean blowing shots to the right that makes the 384-yard hole a lot longer than it seems. There's a lot of trouble on the left, and misses to the right will lengthen the hole. A long par 3 of 198 yards greets you after the 11th, but I found this hole inviting, as there is little trouble here except for the vagaries of the wind. The opposite is true for the 163-yard, par-3, 15th hole, which plays uphill almost always into the wind. The wind can play havoc with the tee shot, especially if it is blowing off the ocean from left to right. Any shot hit to the right will have to carry a gigantic bunker and may be difficult to hold the green. Bandon's greens can be crusty and hard, and sometimes you think you are putting on the moon. The 16th hole is a 363-yard, par 4 with a chasm to carry, fairway, a sandy ridge, more fairway to the tiny green—it is a real wake-up hole on this interesting back nine. A long-hitter can drive this green in downwind conditions. The day ends coming into the clubhouse with a 548-yard, par 5. A generous fairway provides a "welcome back" to what has a spectacular round.

If you love golf, you simply have to get here and have this experience.

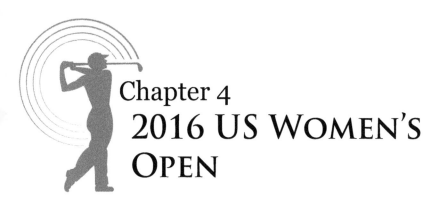

Chapter 4
2016 US WOMEN'S OPEN

ANOTHER USGA RULES DEBACLE

In Golf Chronicles, I have written a chapter of the horrible situation in which Dustin Johnson lost the PGA Championship at Whistling Straits after incurring a penalty for grounding his club in a bunker, which didn't appear to a bunker. The USGA did it to Johnson again in 2016 at the US Open at Oakmont, telling him that he "might incur" a stroke penalty after he caused his ball to move on the 12th green after he addressed it. At that point, Johnson had a one-stroke lead. Many players would have "gone to pieces" with this knowledge, but Johnson had seen the movie before. This time he wasn't going to let the USGA get to him and deprive him of the championship. He summoned up superior skills that Sunday, particularly with the driver, as he went on to win the tournament by three shots. Oh yeah—the USGA decided after the round to assess the penalty anyway, in true absurd fashion.

On to the US Women's Open at Cordevalle Golf Club in San Martin, California, where the USGA would strike yet again.

As a member of Cordevalle, I was able to see the preparations and hoopla leading up to the event. Ian and I played our last round together on Father's Day there. The course would be closed a week later to play, as course preparations would be finalized. Ian plays about six rounds a year: Thanksgiving Friday, Father's Day, my birthday, Final Four Weekend, and maybe once during the Christmas holidays. Despite this lack of play, he continues to play at a high level, which is maddening and terrific at the same time. However, on this Father's Day, I actually beat him, but I didn't "crow" about it. I just came home with a cheshire grin on my face, and Linda knew the result.

The LPGA women started to show up and begin their practice rounds. They would be playing the course from about 6,700 yards, which is typically the same yardage that we play from. The women have a terrific game, which is easier for amateurs such as myself to emulate and admire, than their professional counterparts. Their swings are grooved and a key technique for them is their tempo with slow backswings that allow club head acceleration and speed through the ball. Their technique looks effortless, but they are able to extract a lot of power through the ball.

The club did a terrific job with organizing the event, and the course was ready for the test. In summer, morning tee times can yield low scores, since there is little to no wind and greens are receptive to iron shots, especially with the capability of these women. Temperatures are cool, in the high fifties to low sixties, potentially without sunshine. In the afternoon, the course becomes a completely different animal. The sun comes out in late morning, and the fairways start to run faster, which can impact club selection as greens start to dry out. By noon, the sun is starting to beat down and temperatures rise to the mid-80s. It's by then when the wind starts to blow and all of a sudden, the course turns into a monster. Greens dry up as well as birdie putt opportunities. The leader shot 8 under par on the first day after playing in the morning and took advantage of those conditions. We all knew that 8 under par for the first day would not hold up when considering the players would have to play "both" courses during the week—the morning and the afternoon course.

By the end of the third round, the leader board was bunched up, and at least 10 players had a shot at the title. Lydia Ko, the world's No. 1 player, had a slim lead, but she would have to play flawlessly in the final round to take the title. The players that made the fewest mistakes would emerge as contenders for the title. After making a birdie on the 6th hole, she approached the 8th hole, a straightforward par 3 for these ladies, but the wind conditions started to kick in and her tee shot was deeper than she wanted. She couldn't get up and down from the back fringe and ended up with a bogey.

She proceeded to the most difficult hole on the course: the 565-yard, par-5, 9th hole. The hole is the regular No. 1 handicap hole on the course. You have to cross two hazards. The first hazard is 280 yards from the tee with severe rough on the left and trees and more hazards on the right. Its important to get the tee shot in position for another long iron or wood to position the crossing of the next hazard. The hazard on the left runs all the way down the left side with a tree at the end to block an approach shot, so the second shot has to be hit to the right center of the fairway. Lydia hit her tee shot relatively short into the left rough and had a miserable lie. She had hit the tee shot only about 200 yards and had 130 yards to cross the first hazard. In all cases, I would have laid up to the first hazard, but Lydia decided she could cross the hazard with a hybrid club. She plunked the shot into the hazard and was now facing a big number, and she made double bogey 7 and now her lead was gone. Anna Nordqvist and Brittany Lang were playing steadily and not making mistakes. Other players were following but couldn't make anything happen—the course was not going to yield birdies in the heat, wind, and stress of the competition.

Nordqvist and Lang survived the competition and finished tied for the lead, and therefore a 3-hole playoff would commence to decide the championship. A very exciting conclusion was in store—however, the USGA would strike again.

Play would commence on the par-3 16th hole, and both players made par. On the 17th hole, Nordqvist drove her tee shot into the left bunker, which is about 270 yards. Lang was in the fairway at about the same distance. Nordqvist hit a great shot from the bunker, which landed in the left rough by the green. She was able to get up and down for par, and Lang did the same. Off to the 18th hole—here's where the tragedy begins…Fox Sports Television, who was broadcasting the event live, showed a replay of Nordqvist's bunker shot and revealed a horrible problem. Nordqvist club made contact with an infinitesimal grain of sand so small that no one could have seen it if they were standing behind her. The tape was now being reviewed by the USGA and Nordqvist was going to be assessed a two-shot penalty for making contact with the sand. Meanwhile, both ladies kept playing, not knowing what had occurred and what the consequences would be. The USGA should have stopped play until they decided. It was obvious that this "grain of sand" was going to cost Nordqvist a two-shot penalty. Nordqvist then played her third shot into the 18th green without knowing what was about to occur.

After she hit her shot on the 18th green, the USGA official came up to her and told her that she was being assessed a two-shot penalty for what had occurred on the 17th hole. Crestfallen, Nordqvist accepted her fate, but the USGA should have informed her before she hit that third shot, since she would have known she would have had to make birdie to have any chance to continue the playoff. To make matters worse, the USGA official then informed Lang, before she hit her third shot, that Nordqvist had just incurred a two-shot penalty on 17 and that she was two strokes ahead in the play-off. Lang had a significant unfair advantage, since she knew, before she hit that third shot, that she had a two-shot lead and now all she had to do was put that shot on the green and putt out for the championship, which was what she did. It is amazing how the USGA manages these situations as custodians of the game. Even worse, the USGA president, during the award ceremony, misread Lang's name at least three times—Beverly Lang ?, Bonnie Lang? —How about Brittany Lang!

This type of nonsense should stop. The USGA is responsible to referee the match—not Fox Sports, not Joe Golf Rules Nut sitting in his living room. There should be no "calling it in." Golfers call rule violations on themselves. Nordqvist couldn't have seen that grain of sand in her backswing. If the USGA wants to use video replay of their own to referee the tournament, then they can do what Major League Baseball does: have officials watching the game from afar, or in this case, at the tournament site. There were probably many other "grains of sand" encountered throughout the tournament, but they weren't recorded on Fox Sports. Nordqvist may never get another chance at a US Open victory and this was a terrible way to lose it.

In May 2017, it happened again in an LPGA event. Lexi Thompson was penalized a total of four strokes for not marking her ball properly on the putting green. Without realizing her supposed error, she putted out and then signed her scorecard. A television (couch potato) viewer called in and suggested that Lexi had mismarked her ball on the green, and officials using high-speed cameras determined that the ball was indeed mismarked. Lexi was assessed a two-shot penalty for that error and then assessed another two-shot penalty for signing an incorrect scorecard. The infraction wasn't discovered the next day after she had signed her scorecard. She went on to lose the tournament in a playoff.

The outrage over this penalty was experienced throughout the golf world and was damaging to the sport. The United States Golf Association ("USGA") and the Royal and Ancient Golf Association ("R&A") reacted to this situation swiftly. These governing bodies of the sport reacted with common sense and decided how much video evidence can influence rules decisions at televised events. The new procedure, which is not a new rule, but a new decision (34-3/10) to the Rules of Golf, limits the use of advanced video technology such as high-definition or super- slow-motion cameras in making rulings.

While the procedure is a good decision, it still doesn't address the big-picture issue. I believe that the television-viewing public should never be able to influence rules officials at a televised event. The responsibility of all rules decisions should lie with the tournament officials and match referees who follow the players in a professional event. No other sport allows the television viewing public to influence a ruling in a professional event.

The new procedure focuses on the use of technology for enforcing the rules of golf, rather than defining the people that are responsible for compliance with the rules. Both points should have been addressed, and my vote would be to eliminate anyone not associated with the tournament from having any influence in rules enforcement. The USGA stated that "the new decision would limit the use of video when it revealed evidence that could not be reasonably seen with the 'naked eye' or when players used their 'reasonable judgment' to determine a specific location when performing certain tasks like replacing a marked ball on a green." The "naked eye" standard could be applied to the plight of Anna Nordqvist. I was watching the tournament live at the event and could not detect the infraction standing 15 yards from her, and neither could Nordqvist.

Another example of the "reasonable judgment" standard cited in the statement referred to conditions where a player was putting a ball back in play or determining the nearest point of relief. Tournament contestants usually seek the judgment of the rules official covering the group to ensure that the "drop" or relief point is in conformance with the Rules of Golf. The statement went further and stated that "so long as the player does what can be reasonably expected under the circumstances to make an "accurate determination," the player's judgment will be accepted, even if later shown to be inaccurate through the use of video evidence. The player should not be held to the "degree of precision" that can sometimes be provided by video technology.

Despite the new procedure, the USGA and the R&A didn't stamp out the couch potatoes. It makes me wonder who these people are who believe they should be imposing penalties on players who have exercised judgment believing they did the right thing. The integrity of the Game of Golf is all -important, because the player enforces it. The Rules of Golf provide the background as to how a player complies with the rules, but compliance is still the responsibility of the player.

The USGA and the R&A are forming a working group from the various professional tours and the PGA of America to begin a comprehensive review of video issues, including television viewers who call in to report rules violations in competitions. It seems that such a working group really is unnecessary. The Rules of Golf should specifically prohibit any external influence outside of tournament officials and match referees to determine how the rules should be applied in any set of circumstances. Until these topics are addressed and recommendations delivered to the governing bodies, the television viewer can still call in, except now the influence of that call will not be impacted by evidence from super-slow-motion cameras and video. The "reasonable judgment" and "naked-eye" standards will prevail.

Chapter 5
INTERNATIONAL EXPERIENCES

OLD THORNS, SURREY, ENGLAND

It was a rainy Sunday in England and I wanted to get in a game of golf in 1991. We had just completed a series of business reviews, and Linda and I had a dinner engagement with our friends who were living in Haslemere. Our controller was visiting from the US, and although he wasn't a keen golfer, he agreed to join me to play on that Sunday. My friend made a reservation for me at a course in Surrey called Old Thorns, which I had never played before. Old Thorns seemed to be a public golf course, but it was hard to tell; since the weather was so bad, there weren't many people on the premises. Undaunted, we turned up in the pro shop, and the rain was now teeming. Old Thorns was a parkland course without significant reputation, so this was just going to be an easy routine bonus round.

The rain looked ominous as the professional greeted us and asked us if we really were going to go out into this weather. It was pouring, but it still looked doable with an umbrella, as there didn't seem to be a lot of wind. I should have realized that something was up, since no one else was heading out to the course. . We started out on the first hole as the rain had actually subsided a bit, which gave me a bit of encouragement. I was playing very well, making par after par. It was an easy course—pretty straightforward, with generous tree-lined fairways. My partner was struggling and not having a very good time, and the rain became heavier as we completed the 9th hole; I was even par for the nine with one birdie, one bogey, and seven pars. The rain was making my partner miserable, and we were soaked, as we had no rain gear for this outing. We went into the clubhouse and decided to have lunch and try to dry our clothes. We hung our jackets up by the fire and proceeded to have a hot bowl of soup. This felt really good, and nothing was uttered about proceeding to the back nine. Finally, I piped out that we had to continue since I was having one of the best rounds of my life.

My partner stated emphatically, "I'm done, I've had enough, It's no fun out there."

I immediately protested and said, "It's not bad—and besides, I have to see what I can shoot on the back nine, so I have to get back out there."

My partner said, "I'm done. I'll hold the umbrella for you and you can see what you can do out there."

I was pleased as we headed back out after being inside for over an hour. Normally, you might miss some tempo and good swing thoughts after this type of layover, but I went right back at it and came to the 17th still at even par. It was unbelievable, as the rain continued to come down and the course was beginning to take on water, with puddles developing on the green. The grips on the clubs were now totally gone, and I had little feeling left in my hands. As I took my backswing with my driver on the 17th, I could feel the club begin to slip, and it went flying out of my hand. The club went flying as if it were a drone taking off for the first time. It landed some 100 yards away over the barbed-wire fence that guarded the fairway from a cattle pasture. The ball was hit right down the middle but no more than 125 yards. The biggest problem now was to retrieve the driver, since this was a rental set of clubs. I had to crawl under the barbed-wire fence to retrieve the driver in a sea of mud and leaves, which took over twenty minutes to complete. The rain picked up in intensity to make the situation even worse. I managed to make a bogey on this hole, and I was a mess for the final hole and bogeyed it as well for a two over 74. I was a mess and in need of some clean clothes, especially for our upcoming dinner appointment. My partner couldn't believe that I endured these elements and thought that I should have my head examined. It was a story that he would repeat around the company for many years—witnessing a great round of golf that should have never been played or started. The professional at Old Thorns couldn't believe it either, especially the score for the day. I didn't tell him what happened on the 17th

Brian Shirley's Round at the Old Course at St. Andrews

For many years, a group consisting of myself, Brian and two friends would play golf for a week. We would alternate venues-one year in the US and the next year in Europe and so forth. One of the years, we went to Scotland to play and the venues were Turnberry, Western Gailes, Gleneagles and the Old Course as well as the Jubilee Course at St. Andrews.

We had a 7:00 a.m. tee time at the Old Course, and we were up very early as our drive from Gleneagles to the Old Course was a little over an hour now made even more complicated by the rain that was pouring down. We arrived at St Andrews, and the weather was getting worse. The rain was now horizontal, and the wind was howling. It would be impossible to use an umbrella, so it was Gor-Tex rain gear with a few pairs of golf gloves and towels to negotiate the elements. In addition, I had an envelope from the travel golf company to give to the starter. These days, tee times on the Old Course are precious, so the envelope actually contained an amount of pounds sterling that the travel arranger had "bribed" the starter with so that his customers could play the Old Course. Obviously, the name of the travel arranger shall forever remain anonymous, but I was pretty disturbed by all of this. We had come all this way, and the weather was the worst I had ever experienced playing golf. One of the features of the Old Course is that you must hit the ball left; all the trouble and the gorse bushes are on the right. It was raining so hard that I had to play without my glasses on, so I had the group direct me to the left, where I just continued to hit the ball all day. I played respectably that day, with a round of 83 in the pouring rain. I knocked one of my tee shots on the 14th hole over a wall onto the Jubilee Course. The ball was still in bounds, so I climbed the wall onto Jubilee and played on.

The story of this day would be Brian Shirley. He played meticulously, as if it were a bright sunny day. The wind and rain seemed to have no impact on any of his shots. They just flew straight and crisp through all the elements, as if it were a routine walk in the park. I asked him years after the end of this round what was going through his mind as he approached playing in these elements. Brian was born and raised in Troon, Scotland and had been playing golf since he was seven at Royal Troon. He had a lot of experience in playing in all types of weather, but he was now in mid-sixties, so this was clearly a different situation. His approach to the elements was to neutralize them through focus on his swing plane and trying to strike the ball in the middle of the club. Throughout the day the rain bore down on his Gore-Tex raingear, but he had so much momentum from the first few holes, he was now dialed in and he continued to hit greens in regulation and make pars. He came to the 17th hole, the Road Hole, and crushed another drive down the middle of the 460-yard, par-4 hole. The rest of us were just trying to survive as the rain continued to pour down and the wind was making it hard to see. His approach shot to the green was about 20 yards short, and he had to settle for a bogey. He went round in 77, and we still talk about this round to this day. The weather never improved, and when we had finished and gone in, the starter said, "Not even the locals would go out on a day like today; if you want to play again, you can play for free." This statement came from the same guy who was the recipient of the envelope on the first tee. We politely responded, "No thank you, we're quite done."

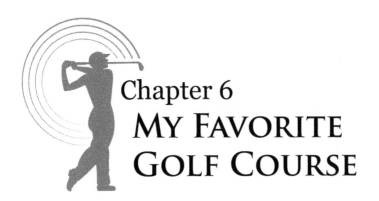

Chapter 6
MY FAVORITE
GOLF COURSE

ROYAL LYTHAM & ST. ANNES,
LANCASHIRE, ENGLAND

Royal Lytham & St. Annes is my favorite course, although I've played it only four times over the years. Brian and I would usually play it in conjunction with a visit to Royal Birkdale and Formby (a great course that has hosted the British Amateur). I like Lytham for a number of different reasons. Unlike many other British private clubs that are on the Open Championship circuit, Lytham welcomes its visitors with a bit of enthusiasm without all the do's and don'ts signs cluttering up the Car Park. You can stay at Lytham in the Dormy House overnight, which is modest, but the rooms overlook the course, which creates a "home" type of experience without a lot of luxurious features after you have had a nice meal at the club's restaurant.

The course is unusual, in that it starts with a 194 yard par 3. Ian Woosnam was victimized in the 2000 Open Championship with a two-stroke penalty for having too many clubs in his bag. His caddy mistakenly had put an additional driver in the bag, and it was quite a scene. Woosnam would become unnerved by the penalty and would not contend for the championship. The front nine of Lytham is a series of very interesting holes that hug the rail line. As you get to the 9th hole, you could drop off your laundry at the dry cleaner's, as the hole is right in the center of the village.

There are 204 bunkers on Lytham. You must hit the ball to the right place; well-connected shots that are not in the right place are likely to be swallowed by these bunkers.

The holes seem to get harder as you get to the house. The 17th hole is particularly treacherous, with the bunkering designed to receive a good tee shot. Adam Scott lost the 2012 Open Championship with a double bogey on this hole. The 18th hole is a classic, with a number of bunkers on either side of the hole with great length and a very large green. When you're putting to win the Open Championship, it's quite intimidating.

I selected Lytham as my favorite because of the variety of the holes, the ambience of the club, and the fairness of what is a solid test of golf.

WHEAT HILL GOLF CLUB—SOMERSET, ENGLAND

Wheat Hill Golf Club is a British private club in Somerset,

England and is Brian's home course. I have been extremely critical of private British golf courses for a number of different reasons. Wheat Hill represents a typical local club in rural England where golf is inexpensive and intensely local. Somerset is a beautiful part of England nestled in Southwest England, bordering Gloucestershire and Bristol to the north and Devon in the southwest. Somerset is a dairy-farming and cattle-raising area, so the land is rich and fertile. The Wheat Hill Club is nestled in the middle of a number of dairy- and cattle-farming locations. The golf course is easy to play, but it has enough teeth to provide an interesting challenge. Wheat Hill is a course that is a great venue to hone your game. It's a confidence-builder for me, and it's possible for me to score around par here if everything is going well. The course is laid out over 6,000 yards of Somerset meadows and tranquil settings. There a number of very strong holes here—the par 3's are short holes and are the reason for the shortness of the course. The par 3's are weak holes and par or better is a must if you want to go low, because the rest of the course presents a pretty good challenge.

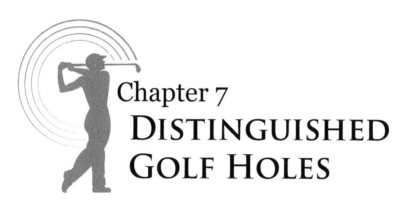

Chapter 7
DISTINGUISHED GOLF HOLES

This section depicts another version of the hardest, most enjoyable and worst golf holes I have ever played.

These are the holes that made significant impressions on my experiences at these wonderful golf venues.

HARDEST HOLES

The hardest holes that are selected here may not be the hardest for other more seasoned and better players, particularly long hitters, but these are the ones that stand out in my experience.

NO. 1—THE ISLAND GOLF CLUB, DUBLIN IRELAND

The first hole on any golf course should be relatively benign, to welcome the player to the experience he is about to encounter. I found most of the opening holes to have these characteristics, with the notable exception of Spyglass Hill in Pebble Beach, which was my selection in my first book, *Golf Chronicles*. The Island Club is located across the channel from North Dublin (Malahide). The course was established in 1890 and isn't very well known outside of Dublin. The course is surrounded by the Irish Sea on three sides and has a rugged beauty. Before the new clubhouse was built in 1973, golfers used to be ferried to The Island from Malahide. It reminded me somewhat of Ballybunion in the South. We had selected Island to play by chance as we were on a holiday to play in the Dublin area. We had the first tee time of the day at 8:00 a.m., and we had no idea of what to expect. Fortunately, a single member of the Club turned up and asked if he could join us. Fred O'Grady was a retired optician, and this was indeed a miracle from the Lord himself. I don't know how we would have gotten around Island without him.

The first hole is "Partridge Hollow," a par 4 of 384 yards. As you approach the first tee, you are immediately intimidated (I certainly was) by the huge mounds, bordering the fairway and the rough, which had to be past our knees. The fairway is extremely tight for a long par 4, and I would estimate it to be no more than 15 yards wide. A missed fairway will lead to a lost shot, as it is impossible to advance the ball very far in this thicket of rough. The drive has to be long enough for a short iron, as the fairway actually narrows at the 270-yard mark off the tee. If you are farther back, you will have to hit a layup shot to the 75-yard mark to try to get up and down for a par. This is the most difficult hole that I ever played that doesn't have a bunker on it.

No. 2—The Riviera Country Club, Los Angeles, California

The second hole at Riviera is a monster par 4 of 471 yards (505 yards at the professional tee box). You have just played the easiest hole on the course, which is the par-5 first hole, and your confidence is high. Now you encounter probably the most difficult hole on the course, which can treat you like a nasty slap in the face. The tee shot has to be long and straight down the fairway. What makes the hole even more difficult is that the prevailing wind off the Pacific Ocean is against making the hole play even longer. The left side is buttressed by a series of trees and must be avoided to have a decent shot to the green. The right side of the hole is even worse and has out of bounds to the driving range (similar to the 12th at Royal Birkdale). The second shot will be a wood, hybrid club, or long iron to the green. You simply cannot be past the pin, as you will have a downhill putt that will be very difficult to judge. The elevated putting surface is situated beneath the clubhouse. Very deep bunkers, whereby it will be very difficult to extricate yourself from the bunker to anywhere near the hole, also guard the green. This is yet another hole where a good approach shot may get a very bad bounce and end up in the bunker or past the pin. A par on this hole is a remarkable event for most players.

No. 3—Cordevalle Golf Club

Not only is this a very difficult hole, it must be praised for its design and the use of the land. If you were looking down from the sky over the hole, you would see that the hole is flanked on the right side by a creek that adjoins the green side of the 1st hole. That stream continues through the middle of the fairway and then snakes up the left side of the hole and through the middle of the fairway again at the green. The stream continues through the right side of the green and continues into the 18th hole. I believe it was a very creative use of the land. The designer has now put so many hazards on this hole that it's hard to enumerate or describe all of them. The hazards will come into play only on shots that are not placed in the fairway. Any shot not placed in the fairway will mostly result in a minimum of one additional stroke. Playing the hole requires a well-thought-out strategy and execution of that strategy.

The first hazard is off the tee box. Depending on the tee box being played, the first hazard is in the middle of the fairway at 240 yards from the forward tee and 290 yards from the championship tee. The player must decide how far to hit this first shot in order to prepare for the short to the second hazard in front of the green. Most likely, depending on the skill of the player, the shot will be a 3 wood to a long iron. If those shots are executed, the last task will be to cover the last hazard and be able to place the ball in the right position for a birdie opportunity. Most par 5's demand one or two well placed shots; this one demands three good shots.

Any shots not in the fairway will result in pain and

suffering for the player. Some examples:

If you miss the fairway and hit the shot into the left rough, you will have to decide whether to lay up to the first hazard or try to carry it. Lydia Ko, during the final round of the 2016 US Women's Open, missed her tee shot into the left rough. She decided to cross the first hazard with a hybrid club—she only needed 135 yards to carry the hazard, but the lie in the rough was horrible. The rough snarled the hybrid, and she experienced the hard lesson: the ball went right into the hazard, and she ended up with a double bogey 7, which was the beginning of the end for her in that championship.

If you miss the fairway and hit the shot of the right side, you will have to contend with oak trees that block the fairway, and any attempt to cross the first hazard brings the treacherous left slope into play.

The best idea is to lay up, take your punishment, and try to make a bogey.

No. 3—Dunes Course at Monterey Peninsula Country Club-Monterey, California

The redesigned Dunes Golf Course at Monterey Peninsula Country Club has been a remarkable achievement, taking a course that was very good and making it great. Criticism of the course prior to the renovation was that the opening holes were rather boring par 4's. The third hole has become one of the most difficult, if not the most difficult, hole on the course. It is a strong par 4 of 374 yards that plays longer than its yardage. Length off the tee is very important, and the fairway is generous, with bunkers guarding the left side of the fairway. Although the hole is straight away, the hole itself is on the right side, so the tee shot should be in the middle or right side of the fairway. The tee shot will determine strategy for playing the rest of the hole. The hole is a gradual climb to the green, so the second shot has to be accurate, since trouble lurks everywhere. Menacing bunkers on the right side, fronting the green, guard the green. The approach shot that misses left even by a yard will present some interesting problems. The left side of the green slides away with a similar look to the greens at Pinehurst No. 2, leaving a chip shot that is very difficult to get up and down. Missing left by too much will make for an impossible chip shot to get close or even make the green. A shot hit over the green will also create havoc, since chipping back to the green is not simple to get close. The green is huge, so the potential for three-putting looms ominously, as the green has many humps and swales. I simply don't have the length off this tee to have a decent shot at the green, so I tend to play it as a par 5. I try to hit my approach shot to the 75-80-yard mark to give my short game the opportunity to pitch it close. Pars are a rare event for me on this hole, and I don't think I'm alone in this endeavor, as the hole is the No. 2 handicap hole on the course.

NO. 4—SPYGLASS HILL GOLF CLUB, PEBBLE BEACH, CALIFORNIA

After you've struggled through the first three holes at

Spyglass Hill, up comes the short par 4 of 345 yards. The tee box gives you a great view of the Pacific Ocean on your left and is the last hole on Spyglass on the ocean, as from here on in, the course turns inward into the Del Monte forest. This hole demands two good shots where club selection and strategy are critical to survival. The hole is a dogleg left, where the tee shot must carry the sand dunes that separate the tee box from the fairway. The sand dunes dominate the entire left side of the fairway, and the long hitter who tries to carry the entire length of the dunes had better find the fairway or else. An attempt to carry the dunes will require an accurate tee shot of 280-290 yards on the fly to have a short pitch shot to the green—not recommended. The rest of us mere mortals must hit this narrow fairway to carry about 190 yards with a three wood, hybrid, or even a long iron. Any drive that is too long will find the ice plant that borders the right side of the fairway. Hitting a shot out of the ice plant is also not recommended. The ball could be sitting in a perfect lie and it appears to be an easy shot. It is a fallacy to think this way, as the ice plant is like hitting out of a thicket of rubber bands. A tee shot into this fairway will give the player an opportunity to find the green with a short iron anywhere from a 7, 8, or 9 iron depending on the distance. The green is extremely narrow. and the best play is to approach the green in the front without attacking the pin. The green slopes front to back with some undulation whereby a shot hit past the hole will release to the back of the green and may find a well-placed bunker in the back of the green. From the back of the green, the putt will be uphill and slide to the ocean. If you find the bunker, the bunker shot will be uphill toward the pin, and a poor bunker shot with too much spin may not make the undulation of the green and cause the ball to spin right back into the bunker. There is simply no way out on this hole, and birdies are possible for two accurate shots, but the dreaded "other" may also happen if you miss this green either right or left, as the hole is surrounded by a thicket of rough, gorse-like material that will ensure at least a bogey or worse.

My experience on this hole has been varied. I once made a 13 on the hole after a drive through the fairway found the ice plant and was sitting up nicely. I decided to hit a 7 iron out of the ice plant, thinking that I could make it to the front of the green some 150 yards out. After 4 swipes of the club, the ball ricocheted off the ice plant and didn't even move. I was incredulous as the fifth shot trickled into the fairway. My 8-iron shot found the back bunker, and my first bunker shot was hit cleanly with too much spin and released back into the bunker. After extricating myself from the bunker and at least 3 putts, I recorded a 13 on this hole. I was a total wreck, as my round was completely trashed at the 4th hole. During another round at Spyglass, I made a birdie here and wanted to walk off the course in absolute celebration. Kudos to designer Robert Trent Jones, Jr. for a hole that is truly unique in my many years of golfing experience. I've never encountered a short par 4 similar to this one in all my years of experience on the golf course.

No. 5—Cordevalle Golf Club, Par 4, 429 yards

I may be a partisan supporter of northern California golf, but the 5th hole is truly a hard hole. The hole vacillates between being either the No. 1 or No. 2 handicap hole on the course. The hole isn't particularly intimidating, but it takes two very good shots to reach the green. (The back tee measures out at 504 yards.) The fairway is wide enough, but there is a bunker that is almost 35 yards long if you miss the tee shot to the right. It will take a drive of 280 yards to clear that bunker on the right, and this capability doesn't exist in my bag. I choose to play the tee shot down the middle and perhaps have 200 yards to the green. Unfortunately, I don't have that shot in my bag either, because the fairway gradually inclines as you get to the green, and therefore makes the second shot almost 20 yards longer than the yardage. The incline makes club selection difficult, as many players play the yardage and come up short to the green or face 60-foot putts to this huge green. Designer Robert Trent Jones, Jr. remembered players like me and placed a huge bunker about 75 yards from the hole that can catch an errant second shot. The green is guarded on the right by a bunch of spinachy rough, and a green side bunker on the right. Pars can be made more easily if the pin is placed on the left side of the green, where approach shots move from right to left on a line that is more appealing to the eye. Pin positions in the center or the right are devilish, with mounding and subtle breaks at the hole itself. Bogey is the routine score for me on this hole, and even the long hitter will struggle to make a par.

NO. 6—WESTERN GAILES GOLF CLUB, PAR 5, 498 YDS., NORTH AYRSHIRE, SCOTLAND

Western Gailes is the finest and truest example of a links golf course that I have ever played. The definition of a links golf course refers to an area of coastal sand dunes and sandy soil unsuitable for farming, but the land supports various different types of bent and fescue grasses. The result supports firm turf, which enables the golf ball to "run" down the fairway. Normal seaside grasses protect the course, chock full of gorse and vegetation that you have to stay away from if you are going to score here. The course is a traditional links course with nine holes out, with the Firth of Clyde (sea) on the left and nine holes in adjacent to the front nine.

When I played Western Gailes a number of years ago, there was very little maintenance required for the course itself. The elements of sun, wind, rain, and temperature variation managed to keep the fairways in a very playable state. I'm sure that a greens-keeper is employed here today, but there doesn't seem to be a lot of other staff required to maintain the course. The links layout is only two holes wide. Mother Nature is conducting much of the maintenance. When you add the element of wind, the course that seems easy and playable becomes very hard, where every shot has to be planned and executed to score.

When you play Western Gailes, it has a unique feeling that the difficulty of every hole is about the same. Most golfers understand that almost every golf course has a series of hard holes that are complemented by a series of easier holes.

You don't get that feeling at Western Gailes. Every hole seems to have the same requirements: proper position in the fairway, and proper execution of a shot to the right position on the green or fairway complemented with the same hazardous elements of gorse, bunkering and high rough. You will face the same elements on every hole and some holes may be dotted with a burn in the front of the green or in the fairway. I selected the 6th hole ("Lappock") as one of the hardest holes at 498 yards and a par 5. The hole requires a tee shot into the fairway by aiming for the clubhouse in the distance. There is severe rough and gorse on the right, and a tee shot that is hit too far left will run through the fairway. A long hitter may try to carry the rough and mounding on the right side of the fairway to try to hit the green in two, but it's a high risk, high-reward opportunity. The second shot from the fairway must be accurate and get as close as possible to the two mounds that shape the fairway about 100-120 yards from the green. The player that tries to go for the green must contend with a green that abnormally veers away from the sea with a bunker strategically located 30 yards from the green. This is a strong par 5, and the wind blowing off the sea can play havoc with any approach shot.

No. 7—The European Club, County Wicklow, Ireland

I am a sucker for links courses, and the European Club is one of my favorites in Ireland. Wicklow is about 50 miles south of Dublin on Brittas Bay and designed by Pat Ruddy.

The European Club is a golf course that I believe is for serious golfers also, because it demands so much concentration. It seemed to me to be a grind from start to finish, and while I don't drink alcohol on the golf course, a good flask of Jameson's 18 would be in order. (Pat Ruddy's European Club philosophy was explained at length in a handout provided to all visitors, and Ruddy's writing made it clear that you weren't just playing a golf course but were set to take part in an idea. And that idea was that golf should be golf and played for golf's sake. "Take your clubs, card and pencil, and go out and do battle with a golfscape that requires no artificial adornment." Ruddy further pontificates, "Golf is a game of skill." "We make no apology that the thoughtfulness and inept player may suffer on our links.")

(*A Course Called Ireland*, Tom Coyne, pg. 218)

No truer words could be spoken as we approached the 7th hole. The 7th hole is a par 4 of 450 yards, and you better have your "A" game for this one. The hole is rated as one of the toughest holes in the game. You simply have to hit a good tee shot in the fairway, as both left and right misses are bad. As you step up to the tee box, you are naturally intimidated by the narrowness of the fairway for a hole this long. You also can't miss the plethora of bushes and fescue that exist to catch every miss. There is a sandbank that runs into the fairway through a thicket of reeds. The green is protected by two deep bunkers sculpted by railroad tees. Big numbers and lost balls abound at this hole, but I managed a bogey by sinking a 12-foot putt.

No. 8—Crooked Stick Golf Club, Carmel, Indiana, par 4, 430 yards

Pete Dye designed Crooked Stick Golf Club, and I believe that this course is his best achievement. Dye is noted and criticized a bit for his use of railroad ties, water, and other forms of trickery in some of his other course designs. John Daly won his first major title here at the PGA Championship in 1991. We had a wonderful experience here as we were attending the NCAA Final Four championship in Indianapolis. We were very fortunate to be able to play, because it was Easter Sunday and the club graciously accommodated us. We found a great touch of midwestern hospitality here and we were made to feel very welcome. I didn't have any golf clubs with me, as we usually don't travel with golf clubs to these events. As it was Easter Sunday, there wasn't a lot of staff available, and there could have been a problem since there were no clubs available to rent. The club professional quickly realized and trotted out with his personal clubs and offered them to play for the day's play. I was incredibly grateful that he would do this, and off we went to play the Pete Dye venue. It was very impressive, and there wasn't a soul on the golf course in the afternoon, so we had the course to ourselves. I was also surprised to note that the course rating was 148 (Pine Valley is 155) and I found the course to be very playable and great to play with a combination of easy and difficult holes. The par 4, 420-yard hole is very difficult, as the position of the drive off the tee should be on the right side of the fairway. Due to the length of the hole and the wind in our faces, I had a shot of 200 yards to the green that had to be accurate. The fairway isn't that wide, and there is a huge bunker guarding the green, with water in play on the left all the way to the hole. Bogey was a good score on this hole. It was a wonderful, relaxing day on a great golf course.

NO. 9—OAKHILL COUNTRY CLUB, EAST COURSE, ROCHESTER, NEW YORK

Oakhill's East Course is the iconic course designed by Donald Ross. Oakhill has hosted many events including US Opens, US Amateur Championships, and the Ryder Cup. The ninth hole is 400-yard par 4 nicknamed, "Needle's Eye." The hole is uphill as a dogleg to the right. Courses designed by Ross are very tough for me, because there are a lot of holes that play a lot longer than the stated yardage, as the fairways simply don't advance the ball. This fairway is no wider than 25 yards, and if you miss it, you most likely will have to have the chip the ball back in the fairway. If you could crunch it 260 yards, you'll catch the down slope of the fairway, leaving you a short pitch shot to the green. So why is this hole so hard? Well, there's no way that I could hit the required 260 yards to catch the down slope; the fairway is only 25 yards wide, so it's hard to get it in there, and finally the trees make it even more difficult depending on your spot in the fairway. I hit a pretty decent drive but had an uphill shot of 170 yards and dunked in the bunker and made bogey. "Needle's Eye" is a very appropriate description for this hole.

No. 10—Pine Valley Country Club, Clementon, New Jersey, par 3, 142 yards.

Every hole at Pine Valley would make my hardest list, so I've actually chosen the one that might be the least hard—at least it was for me. Pine Valley is the most difficult golf course on this planet. Designer George Crump, depending on your point of view, is either the devil incarnate or the god of golf course creation. The course is located in Southern New Jersey in the Jersey pines. The course rating for Pine Valley is 155 from the championship tees and 153 from the regular tees. The goal here for me was to break 100, as I would be expected to play here as a 15 handicap which is ten strokes worse than my current handicap of 5. Pine Valley is a very private club and is usually rated the top golf course in the country, and I would say it's the top- rated golf course in the world. This is a course where the fairway is a piece of prime real estate, as the course has almost as much sand and waste areas as fairway. There are so many bunkers and waste areas that there are no rakes in the bunkers. Club management and members do not provide these utensils, because the pace of play would be intolerable. You are simply required to clean up after yourself after you've extricated the shot from these areas. The par-3 10th hole measures 142 yards and is completely surrounded by bunkers, so there is only one place to hit the ball—yes, on the green. However, you may hit this green and have it roll off into one of the horrendous bunkers that surround the hole. There is a bunker in front of the green that you cannot see from the tee box, and if you're playing here for the first time, you won't know it's there despite the warnings from your caddy. This bunker is aptly named "the devil's asshole," or more affectionately, "the bottomless pit." It's highly doubtful that you will make par on this hole from any of these bunkers, as the greens are incredibly fast, measuring 12-13 on the stimp meter.

I took a deep breath approaching this hole and calmly took a seven iron and hit it as high as I could. Of course, the ball carried onto the green but rolled off the backside into one of the less penal bunkers. I did manage to make bogey, and bogey was the operative goal for this hole and the course in general. I shot 95, but it was a tremendous experience; fortunately, I had a few more opportunities to play here. Bring your "A" game to Pine Valley and hopefully break 100. Professionals and capable amateurs rarely get around in par on this course. Pine Valley has a practice layout that is designed to give you a feel for what you are about to encounter, but I simply don't have enough sand shots in one round to master this wonderful place. It's a course that doesn't get a lot of publicity because it's a very private place without any professional tournament play on it. The terrain is unable to accommodate thousands of spectators, and the club has no intention of changing this pristine layout to accommodate crowds, tents, and all the trappings of a professional event.

NO. 11—WINGED FOOT COUNTRY CLUB, WEST COURSE, MAMARONECK, NEW YORK

The Course at Winged Foot Country Club in Westchester County, New York has hosted many major championships and has been a US Open venue on a few occasions. Winged Foot is a pretty difficult track and has a pedigree that places in a similar class as Pine Valley. It's reputed that the membership of Winged Foot has the largest number of single-digit handicaps at any private club in the United States. This is an amazing statistic considering the overall difficulty of the golf course. Most of the holes on the West Course could be selected as very difficult, but I selected the par-4 11th hole, which measures 386 yards. The hole is a straightforward par 4, with trees protecting and shaping both sides of the fairway. The best tee shot should be down the right side of the fairway to get a good angle to the green. The green is large and surrounded on all sides by three bunkers on each side with a subsequent bunker in the back of the green. The bunkers curl up to the front of the green, and getting up and down from these bunkers won't be easy. My last visit to Wing Foot was humbling, as I was playing in a charity event, having just flown in from California. My group was depending on my single-digit handicap for considerable help, but it would not come on this day. It was pouring rain for the entire round, and it took me quite a few holes to demonstrate any level of skill, but I did manage to par in on the final six holes.

NO. 12—TORREY PINES SOUTH COURSE, SAN DIEGO, CALIFORNIA

Torrey Pines is one of the finest public golf courses in the United States and is a jewel on the bluffs of the highlands in San Diego, California. Torrey Pines was the host of the 2007

US Open and was the last major event that Tiger Woods won. The South Course is the tournament course that the Open was played on. One of its strongest holes is the 456-yard par 4. The hole is characterized by a narrow fairway where an accurate tee shot is required, and it will take a drive of over 260 yards to clear the fairway bunkers. The hole is made even more imposing by the prevailing wind, which tends to be in your face. The green is large and flanked by what seems to be very large bunkers. Professionals are satisfied to make par on this hole, as it requires two excellent shots to make the green. The green's undulations are subtle and are breaks are usually around the cup, which makes reading these greens more difficult. I've never made par on this hole for a number of reasons, but it's a hole for the long driver of the ball. This hole usually doesn't decide anything in a tournament setting, but it can be a momentum-buster, as the previous three holes at Torrey are shorter and easier.

No. 13—Druids Glen, Dublin, Ireland

Druids Glen is a parkland course outside of Dublin, which occasionally hosts the Irish Open. It's generally a pleasant walk in the park, with holes that are quite playable and fair. The 13th is a wonderfully designed hole but extremely difficult and challenging for the player who hasn't played it before. The tee is significantly elevated, and the hole is a very long dogleg. A stream that emanates from the 12th and some other holes winds its way in front of the tee and continues all the way down the right-hand side of the fairway. It eventually winds its way all through the right-hand side of the fairway and cuts across the fairway into a man-made lake on the left side of the fairway. The player has a number of different alternatives, but each shot must be precise if a par is to be recorded. The hole measures 451 yards as a par 4. One way to play it is to play it as a par 5 and hope for some magic out of your game. In this manner, you hit a 3 wood off the tee into the center of the fairway. You won't be able to hit it far enough to reach the green in two, as you'll have an approach shot of over 230 yards. So you lay up in front of the stream and have a 160-yard iron shot to go to the green. The shot must be hit perfectly if you are to convert a par on this hole.

Another way to play it is risky; you hit a driver and try to carve it to the right side of the fairway. The drive must be very precise and hit about 265 yards to hit the fairway on the right. Anything missed in yardage or direction will end up in the stream or in impossibly high grass; bad things will happen, and you can forget par or bogey.

I played it the first way and hit a 5 iron from 165 yards in front of the stream to seven feet and made a par. My playing partners didn't listen and lost more than a few balls in the stream and the high grass.

NO. 14—NICKLAUS CLUB, MONTEREY (FORMERLY PASADERA GOLF CLUB)

The 14th at the Nicklaus Club, Monterey, California is the signature hole for the course. The hole is a par 3 of 180 yards from the back tee and 220 yards from the professional tee. You have to clear the 180 yards to make it to a huge green, as your tee shot must carry the gorge/mountain side, as there is nothing between the tee and the green except the ravine. There is a bunker that guards the green about 179 yards from the tee that hopefully will catch a shot that isn't "flushed." The green is immense vertically; I would estimate it to be almost 35 yards in length. The width of the green is probably about 10-12 yards. The green is replete with undulations, making putting very interesting. With a green this large, pin placements abound, with the most difficult pin being on the right side of the green, which is adjacent to the chasm of the ravine. A big problem for the amateur is not only carrying the shot the full 180 yards (or 179 yards into the front bunker) but also keeping the ball on the green. Amateurs generally don't hit the ball as high as they need to on a hole like this one. Professionals and low-handicap amateurs can hit high shots with a 6 or even 7 iron to carry this distance and reach the green. Most amateurs have to hit a 5 iron or a hybrid club to carry the ravine, and these shots have a tendency to be lower and can run through the green. On this hole, however, shots that run through the green will likely meet with a bad ending. Any shot through the green will probably run down the hill into a batch of snarly grasses and exposed roots that will leave the player in a bad mood— especially if the tee shot was hit well but bounced through the green. From over the green in this position, it will be impossible to make par, and the most likely score will be a double bogey. There is a tendency to hit a shot to the left of the green, which seems to be an easier carry, and there is kind of a landing area that makes it possible to get the ball up and down to make a par. The shot from the professional tees is 220 yards and really demands a shot that can carry 200 yards in the air and hit high enough for it to hold the green. Par is possible on this hole, but what makes the hole difficult is that any shot that misses the green and ends up in the ravine will end badly, with a big number recorded.

The Nicklaus Club is about 15 years old, and I was a member here. I used to hit a 7 wood exclusively on this hole to try to produce the high shot of 180 yards and avoid going over the ravine. I have had some reasonably decent experience on this hole, but it certainly is intimidating, with breathtaking views of the Monterey Peninsula.

NO. 15—ROYAL TROON GOLF CLUB, TROON SCOTLAND

I selected the 15th at Royal Troon, as it is the beginning of the way in to the clubhouse. The stretch of holes that begins with the 15th is made difficult by the prevailing wind, which is usually against the player. The hole measures 436 yards as a par 4, and the fairways are well bunkered to catch the drives of professionals and amateurs alike. The best position for the tee shot is the left side of the fairway, avoiding the bunkers. A tee shot that misses the fairway will find rough that can be very penal, depending on the time of year. In summer, the rough can be lower and a bit wispy so the ball can be advanced but unlikely for the amateur to reach the green. I've had it both ways on this hole, with success when the wind is with you during summer, when the ball carries well. I've also made double bogey here by hitting into wet rough with difficult shots to the green. The green is protected by well-placed pot bunkers. It's important to play this hole, as you'll be playing the last three holes in similar windy conditions. The duel between Henrik Stensen and Phil Mickelsen in the 2016 Open Championship produced a lot of great golf on the way in before Stensen finally prevailed as he took a two-shot lead with a long birdie putt on 15.

NO. 16—PASATIEMPO GOLF CLUB

While not mentioned in *Golf Chronicles*, this is a diabolical hole that McKenzie probably licked his chops with this design. The hole is a 377-yard par 4 that demands two "A"-game shots to get to the green to make par. Everything about this hole demands significant precision from the player. The tee shot is blind, but there is a directional marker in the center of the fairway, so no excuses there. The tee shot must be straight and long, or there is no chance to make par and very little chance of hitting the green. The landing area for the tee shot is tiered, so if you hit it long enough, you can reach a flat area in the fairway that will give you an approach shot of 130-160 yards, depending on the position. Any tee shot that is pulled left of the marker is likely to find a graveyard down a hill from which one can one take a "penalty" shot and get the ball back into the fairway. Any tee shot that is shoved to the right of the marker lengthens the hole considerably, with virtually no chance of having a shot to the green. Therefore, misplayed tee shots require layups to the flat fairway area where you will have a shot of 120-130 yards to the green.

So, you've hit a great tee shot and you're now standing in the flat part of the fairway about 150 yards from the hole. Now the fun really begins! The green is absolutely huge, with three tiers. Each tier is significantly sloped, so that any shot to the green can end up at the bottom of the green. I estimate that from bottom tier to top tier is about 25 yards, or 75 feet. If the pin is at the top tier, you have to add at least 20 yards to the shot in the fairway, because you must clear the first two tiers of the green. If you don't, you will end up at the bottom tier and have a 75-foot uphill putt. Realistically, you'll be lucky to three-putt from that position. The green, as large as it is, is covered with enormous bunkers on the left and another on the right. The bunkers definitely are in play for the approach shot to the green, and any shot hit into the right bunker is likely to suffer significant pain and strokes.

A green this large obviously has many pin positions. I've never seen a hole where the pin position dictates so much of the strategy for the approach shot. If the pin is at the top tier of the green, the approach shot must land on the top tier or it will fall precipitously to the bottom. Putting at the top tier position isn't too bad, as the breaks are discernible. The best pin position to make a par or even a birdie on this hole is the middle-tier position. In this position, the approach shot should fly past the hole, where the player can use the slope to get the ball to move toward the pin. Any shot past the hole in this pin position that has a lot of spin can also work well to get into a birdie or par position. This pin position brings the right-side bunker into play, but it is possible to avoid that bunker and get the ball into a decent spot. A very hard pin placement is the left side of the green on the second tier. For this pin placement, the approach shot must be on the second tier, but it has to be level and a smidge past the pin. Any shot hit past this pin position is likely to run on to some very bad places, such as the extreme left of the second tier, which will make putting for par or birdie a low-probability event. Another problem with this pin position is that the left bunker must be carried. Any shot hit into this bunker with this pin position is almost impossible to get up and down.

I don't have the statistics, but I would wager that this hole would have the highest stroke average on the course. It is rated the No. 2 handicap hole, but you can really make some big ugly numbers here.

No. 17—Royal Lytham and St. Annes, Lancashire, England

In *Golf Chronicles*, I described the Road Hole, the 17th hole at the Old Course at St. Andrews, as the hardest 17th hole I had ever played. The 17th at Royal Lytham and St. Annes is a close second. Today the hole has been lengthened to 467 yards (par 4) but irrespective of length, it is a very difficult hole. The hole has 19 bunkers out of the 165 bunkers that dot Royal Lytham and St. Annes. Eight of those bunkers can catch the tee shot, and it is not really possible to carry all of the bunkers. The hole turns left for the green at about the 250-yard mark if you're in the center of the fairway. The real problem with the hole is that you miss the fairway on the left, since there is nothing but sand dunes and a blind shot to the green. If you miss the fairway on the right, the hole will become significantly longer, and par becomes a distant possibility. Six bunkers guard the green, with four on the left and two on the right. The bunkers on the left are well placed to catch a blind shot from the sand dunes. Winds on this hole can swirl off the ocean and add complexity to the approach shot. My goal here was to make a bogey by avoiding the bunkers and keeping the ball out of dunes, and fortunately this was accomplished.

This hole was a "Waterloo" for Adam Scott in the 2012 Open Championship. His tee shot missed the fairway on the left, and his blind second shot came up short; he was unable to get up and down for a bogey that cost him the lead in the Championship that he had held for the last two rounds. Ernie Els claimed victory after Scott bogeyed the 18th hole as well.

In 1926, Bobby Jones won the Open Championship, and it was won on this hole. The hole during that period played to 411 yards, and Jones hit a drive of 236 yards that left him 175 yards to the hole. The problem was that the ball went left into the dunes, leaving Jones with an almost impossible shot. The shot was blind to the green, with all those bunkers in play. The competition at that time was match play, and his opponent's drive was in the middle of the fairway. Jones's lie was essentially sand, and the chance to put the ball on the green was very slim. Jones executed the shot perfectly, and the ball landed closer to the hole than his opponent's. His opponent was shattered by Jones's shot—the match was all square at the time, and he ended up three-putting to lose the hole to Jones, who two-putted for a par. A plaque exists at the site of Jones's shot. In match play, the adage "never underestimate what your opponent can do" was never truer.

No. 18—Yale University Golf Club, New Haven, Connecticut

The 18th hole at Yale is a spectacular finishing hole, measuring 620 yards as a par 5. This hole is a three-shot par 5, irrespective of skill level. The tee shot has to carry the ridge on the right as the tee shot is elevated. A good tee shot on the right will enable the player to hit a long approach shot to set up the second shot, which has to be carefully placed to the middle or the right side. The second shot is also elevated, and a long hitter can get it past the top of the hill toward the green. The approach to the green will be over 170 yards if the second doesn't reach the top of the hill. Anything shot missed to the right will bring trees into play and block approaches to the green. The hole is the end of a long grind of a very difficult golf course that is viewed as the top university golf course in the United States.

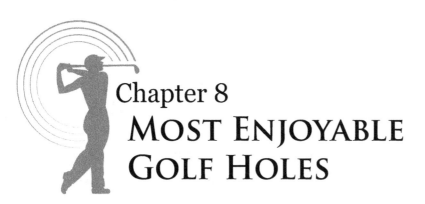

Chapter 8
MOST ENJOYABLE GOLF HOLES

There are so many beautiful golf courses in the world that I present here another edition of the most enjoyable holes that I have played.

NO. 1—SPANISH BAY GOLF LINKS, PEBBLE BEACH, CALIFORNIA

The first hole at the Spanish Bay Golf Links in Pebble Beach, California evokes memories of the Old Course at Saint Andrews. The hole is a par 5 of 505 yards with a generous wide fairway, which can be a confidence-builder to start the round. The first tee is located right next to the starter's location (same as St. Andrews) with a spectacular view of the Pacific Ocean on the right (at St. Andrews, it is the Firth of Forth). The only problem for the high-handicapper is that there is that thought that everybody is watching you tee off so the distraction factor can set in causing some awful results. A good tee shot in the fairway is followed by a long iron or 3 wood to the left side of the fairway for an approach shot of 120 yards or so (maybe less for the long hitter). Any shot hit to the right of the fairway will require a more difficult approach over a patch of horrendous rough, which shouldn't really be in play. The approach shot should be short of the green to bounce onto the green, which is surrounded by the gorgeous ocean view. The green is large and contoured, which makes it difficult to get close to the pin, so the approach demands more accuracy than all of the other shots on the hole. Birdies are possible here, but the landing area on the green must be below the hole for that type of opportunity. The hole is enjoyable to play, as it will reward the good shots and welcome you for the rest of the round at this enjoyable course.

NO. 2-ROYAL DUBLIN, DUBLIN, IRELAND

Royal Dublin's second hole presents the best birdie opportunity on the course. The hole is a par 5 of 467 yards with a gentle dogleg to the right. Of course, they tell you it's a birdie hole, provided the prevailing west wind is actually prevailing. When I played it in October, 2017, the wind was blowing 25 miles with the player. We had no time to hit any practice balls (lame excuse), so my drive on the 2nd went sailing into the rough on the right, leaving a 125-yard shot to the green. The wind makes it hard to hold the green, and any hole in a lateral position on the hole makes it difficult to get up and down for the birdie. My approach shot bounced on the green but didn't hold and I didn't execute a difficult pitch shot, so an early bogey was posted on the card. I had a difficult front nine that day and was pretty annoyed with myself, since the entire 9 holes were downwind. I was pretty crestfallen as I approached the 10th tee into a 25-mph wind. Golf is such an amazing game; the entire back nine was into the wind, but the harder it blew, the better I played, and I came back in just 2 over. The score on the front nine is unprintable. The day was blessed with the eagle putt I had on the 18th hole, as I played the hole completely incorrectly. I smashed a 3 wood out perfectly to the edge of the burn and had 235 yards to the hole coming into the green. I was told the right play would be to avoid the gorse and all the trouble and hit the second shot to the left side of the fairway, leaving a short pitch to the green. The wind was howling, so I didn't pay any attention to what my playing partners were doing and decided to go for the green with another 3 wood from 235 yards out. Any shot short of the green was absolutely dead and probably not findable. I didn't even think twice about this and grabbed the 3 wood and let it rip. The ball carried all the junk and landed on the green some 60 feet from the hole, but a finishing birdie here at Royal Dublin was pretty special.

NO. 3—MAUNA KEA, BIG ISLAND, HAWAII

Mauna Kea is another special spot in the world of golf, earning a spot on the top 100 list. The 3rd hole is the signature hole for the course, as a par 3 measuring 205 yards from the back tee and 179 yards from the regular tee. The hole has a spectacular view, with the ocean on the left side. The tee shot has to carry the entire bay, which translates to a shot of over 200 yards, especially if there is any wind. We played the hole from the regular tees, but of course, we had to take a whack at the hole from the back tees. My 3 wood from the back tee barely carried and ended on the lower part of the green. The green is huge horizontally for a par 3, and most putts are fairly level, with some break toward the ocean. There are seven bunkers on the hole, but only missed tee shots to the right or short can find them. The green is so large and horizontal that shots out of these bunkers are not difficult unless you miss the green to the right, where the bunkers will present a more difficult shot. I had a disappointing three-putt bogey here. There are many good golf holes in Hawaii, but this stands out as the best.

No. 4—Le Pavoniere Golf and Country Club, Tuscany, Italy

I highly recommend playing golf in Italy if you have the time from touring nearby Florence. Golf in Italy is a lot like most things in Italy—very relaxing and rewarding. This is not Scotland or the rugged terrain of Ireland. Golf in Italy is not very popular and is viewed to be a pastime for the rich and aristocratic. What I like about it is that the players might be rich and aristocratic, but they don't act like it and seem to relish the challenge of hitting the golf ball. When you play golf in Italy, it is truly like a stroll in the park—provided you don't have slow players in front of you. There is nothing really difficult about the course, and it was a big ego-booster for me, as I shot 69, or 3 under par, for the 6,131 layout. I selected one of the more challenging holes here—the par-4 4th hole of 358 yards. The hole is bordered by a lake on the right side of the hole that runs from tee to green, so anything hit right will get wet. The tee shot has to be down the left side of the fairway, which is a bit narrow off the tee but then extends out nicely to the left side. Two fairway bunkers are very well placed to catch tee shots that hit right down the middle. It's probably a carry of 240 yards to clear both of these fairway bunkers. As you approach the second shot, the water actually meanders around the green, creating almost an island effect. The second shot has to carry the hazard to get onto the green, which is large but much more horizontal. You can't run the ball through the green, as the water will come into play. I hit a great drive down the left side of the fairway and had a pitching wedge to the green for an easy par on one of the more challenging holes on the course. I birdied 3 of the par 5's and didn't make a bogey all day. This was not my typical round of golf, to be sure, but the ambience of the place made the course both interesting and enjoyable.

No. 5—Dunes Course at Monterey Peninsula Country Club

The 5th at Monterey Peninsula Country Club was completely redesigned as a very short par 4 of 302 yards. The hole was created as a significant risk/reward type of hole. The hole is uphill, but the uphill isn't really in play due to the length of the hole. The green is at a one o'clock position and is drivable. The terrific design element is the well-placed bunker at the 270-yard mark directly guarding the green and meant to catch a tee shot that otherwise might make the green. There are a number of ways to play the hole, which really adds to its enjoyment. There are two trees in the distance, which present the target driving direction—the feeling is like driving the golf ball through the uprights on a football field. The right side of the hall is an enormous waste bunker, which will catch any shot hit to the right. Big numbers can be made out of this bunker, as you're likely to have a bunker shot of at least 120 yards. On the right of the bunker, there is a burn, which runs all the way to the green and beyond. The only thing you can say here is never to hit a tee shot to the right on this hole. Slicers need to aim way left and stay out of this bunker. One approach is to hit a driver or a 3 wood to the left side of the bunker for a pitch shot into the green. Most players just try to drive the green, as it seems to be a very inviting choice. The difficulty of the hole is the green itself as it very large and has a number of humps and contours, so the approach shot must carry the first hump on the green to have any chance of making a birdie. Any pitch shot that carries over the green will produce a very difficult shot coming back. Leaving this hole without a par or a birdie is a very depressing thought.

No. 5-Mannings Heath Golf Club, West Sussex, England

Mannings Heath Golf Club is a semi-private golf club located in West Sussex, England about 50 miles south east of London on the way to Brighton, which is another 60 miles farther south. Mannings Heath is a parkland golf course built on heath land, which provides very generous natural turf and the fairways here are among the best I have ever played. The 5th hole at Mannings Heath is a uniquely designed hole. It is labeled "The Punchbowl." The hole is a par 3 of 164 yards and is played from an elevated tee. Club selection can be variable here due to the wind. The prevailing wind is either against or left to right. The hole is shaped like a bowl, as the mounding surrounding the hole covers 75% of a circle that shapes the bowl. The other 25% is out of bounds to the left into a thicket of trees and scrub brush. A tee shot that reaches the green will be rewarded with a certain par and a potential birdie opportunity, since the green is small and relatively flat. Any shot missed to the right can potentially miss all of the mounding, leaving the player with an awkward chip onto the green ("bowl"). Shot missing the green inside the bowl will have very difficult chips from the thick rough that surrounds this green. This is one hole where one good shot is needed to make par or birdie, and a miss can yield a much higher number.

No. 6—San Lorenzo Golf Club, Algarve, Portugal

San Lorenzo is one of the most scenic places to play in the Algarve, and a place I long to get back to. The Algarve is a mecca for golf and draws a number of vacationers from the UK and Germany. Golf courses in the Algarve tend to be similar with respect to grasses used in the fairways. The greens tend to be a lot slower than US golfers are used to. San Lorenzo was an exception for me and differentiated from most of the courses I played in the region. San Lorenzo has a few holes near the Atlantic Ocean, and low tide produces some additional, if not unwanted, space to hit a golf ball. The par-4 6th hole measures a little over 400 yards, with a dogleg to the left, and the tee shot has to find the fairway. The fairway is wide enough, but it takes a drive of 245 yards to get to the dogleg. At the dogleg, the fairway narrows considerably for the iron shot to the green. A tee shot to the right could find the beach, which runs from the right side of the hole. Shots from the beach are exciting, to be sure, and recovery from the beach is possible provided the tide is out. The green is fairly large for a hole of this size, but I don't find the greens on Algarve courses to be particularly challenging, because they are generally slow, ranging from 8-10 on the stimpmeter. San Lorenzo is a very enjoyable course to play and blends right into the beach culture that is the Algarve.

No. 7—Lundin Golf Club, Largo, Scotland

Lundin is a private club very close to St. Andrews, Scotland in a tiny fishing village called Largo. This is a great place to play after you have maneuvered around the Old Course, New Course and Kings/Barnes. The 7th hole at Lundin is a 266-yard par 4 with ditches that bisect the fairway on either side of the hole. Those ditches should not come into play. The green is raised a bit and is pretty small as you might expect for such a short hole. There is another ditch that completely surrounds the hole along with two bunkers that guards the green. I didn't think it made any sense to try and drive this green as there is too much trouble to deal with—ditch, bunkers, high grass etc. I took a 5 iron and wedge and missed my birdie putt but the hole is just fun to play. Trying to drive the hole might be the "macho" thing to do but my bag doesn't contain drivers that have the capability of driving a green.

No. 8—Royal Troon Golf Club-The Postage Stamp

What can be so special about a 123-yard par 3? There are myriad short par 3's in the world of golf courses. This hole happens to be at Royal Troon in Troon, Scotland. The course has been in the rotation of British Open venues for as long as the championship has been played. When you play Troon on the coast of Scotland, it's as if you're at the end of the world. The quiet is deafening and can be disturbed only by the drone of an occasional military jet landing nearby at Prestwick Airport. As you move to the elevated tee box, there is a bit of trepidation as you survey the shot that you are about to it. The green is extremely small and was aptly named "Postage Stamp" by a British author writing about the hole in a golf magazine in the 1930s. The "envelope" is pretty small, and accuracy is all-important. A gully chock- full of gorse and high grass must be carried, as well as a gigantic bunker that guards the front of the green. This shouldn't be a problem, as club selection is probably an 8 or 9 iron for the average player. There is a bunker on the left called the "coffin" bunker because if you land in it, you certainly will be "dead" and lucky to escape with a bogey. The ball must not only land on the green, but it must land on the left side of the green to have the birdie opportunity. If the pin is at the back of the hole, the player might be a tad more careful, as long as the ball is below the hole.

The green sits just to the right of an immense sand dune and is framed by five bunkers. Two of those bunkers will catch any ball that rolls off a steep slope to the right. The green is only 12 yards wide at the front and only 10 yards wide at the back. The locals also affectionately call the hole "The Wee Beastie." I've had some good luck here at this hole and never made it into one of those bunkers. However, I couldn't say the same for the rest of the course, which seems to get harder after this hole, especially on the way in the prevailing wind that is usually against the player. Phil Mickelson is quoted as saying, "Challenging a player for his precision as opposed to solely length is a lost art." The Postage Stamp is a perfect example.

No. 9—East Lake Golf Club, Atlanta, Georgia

East Lake Golf Club represents the finest tradition in southern hospitality and has hosted many national and regional championships since 1904. East Lake is also the home of the PGA Tour Championship, which has produced quite of excitement during its tenure. The ninth hole is a straightaway par 3 of 207 yards. The tee box is sculpted by ponds on both sides of the fairway. The length of the hole is its strength, as the tee shot has to carry the two large bunkers guarding the entrance to the green. The professional player will probably choose a 5 iron to this green, as the player will be able to get the ball to stop and hold these fast greens. As for me, I needed to belt a 3 wood and hope for the best. I managed to drive the ball into the right bunker and couldn't convert the up and down for a bogey 4.

No. 10—Riviera Country Club, Pacific Palisades, California

The 10th at Riviera is a short par 4 of 325 yards that can really create havoc for the player. Professionals have been beleaguered by this hole for many years, and I'm sure low-handicappers are happy to leave this hole with a par. It's a significant temptation to drive the green, but any miss in this endeavor can result in a very tough pitching position. Strategic bunkering that will test the mettle of any professional surrounds the green. If the tee shot is missed to the left of the hole, there is a grove of menacing trees and rough that will make getting up and down for par a real challenge. My choice to play the hole is to hit a 4 or 5 iron 180 yards to the middle of the fairway, and then take my chances with a wedge to the green. The green has a number of difficult pin positions, so birdies are not easy to come by for such a short hole.

NO. 11—PINEHURST NO. 8, SOUTH CAROLINA

Pinehurst No. 8 is a little-known gem in the Pinehurst resort, as all the courses take a back seat to Pinehurst No. 2, where major championships take place. No. 8 is the second-most-difficult course in the Pinehurst resort and has a number of very interesting holes. The 11th hole is a par 5 of 574 yards, and the fairway slopes left to right. What is great about playing golf in the southeast of the United States is that the fairways run, and driving distance can be enhanced by the cuts of the fairways. On this hole, what you see is what you get, and if you can place the ball on the left side of the fairway, you can hit your second shot to the right side of the fairway to avoid all the bunkers and plan your approach shot to a slightly elevated green. There is plenty of room to execute these shots and get the ball on the green in regulation. On this course and all of the Pinehurst venues, putting is usually the most difficult part of the green, as you have to be able to make out the undulations and follow the grain to get the right speed. The 11th was a breath of fresh air for me, as I recorded an easy par on one of the easier holes on the course. It was a confidence-builder for what was to follow on No. 8.

NO. 12—THE EUROPEAN CLUB, WICKLOW, IRELAND

No. 12 at the European Club is really hole 12A. Pat Ruddy's design of the golf course is actually 20 holes. The idea was that the player could choose to play either hole at 12—or perhaps it was necessary for maintenance reasons to close one of the holes. You can also play the 20 holes on the course at par 78. I actually played 12 and 12A, but 12A was special, in that it seemed to be the actual inverse of a hole at Tralee. This hole is longer than the one at Tralee, at 203 yards, with the Atlantic Ocean on the left providing a breathtaking sight from the tee box. Like the hole at Tralee, there is no place to miss, as there is considerable mounding that will put you in harm's way if you're short. Coffin-like bunkers must be avoided to get a par here. I was lucky here, as there was little wind to toss the ball around, and I was able to reach the green with a hybrid club and managed a par 3.

NO. 13—TRALEE GOLF CLUB, TRALEE, IRELAND

The 13th at Tralee Golf Club is a par 3 of 150 yards, but the view of the hole is breathtaking and intimidating at the same time. At Tralee, the saying is that "Arnold Palmer designed the front but God designed the back nine." The par 3 is all carry over the gorge of native grasses. The tee shot offers some area to the right, but the yardage still needs to be carried. Any shot that is short or pulled left will find its grave at the bottom of the gorge. The hole is sculpted by large mounds through the green. A shot through the green will be very difficult to get up and down to make a par. No bunkers on this hole, but there is certainly plenty of everything else to intimidate the player.

No. 14—Florence Golf Club, Ugolino, Florence, Italy

An Englishman and an Irishman utilizing the slopes of the Tuscan hills designed Florence Golf Club. The course is not long, but it's pretty difficult, as the fairways are narrow and the course meanders through a series of slopes bounded by vines, olive trees, and maritime pines. I played Ugolino for the first time in 2012, and the travel agent was aghast that I would want to play golf in Italy, especially while touring Florence and Tuscany. My driver picked me and brought me through the long, winding drive up to the clubhouse. It actually reminded me of driving up Magnolia Lane at Augusta National. Unfortunately, the rental set of clubs they gave me would not have survived a week in my garage. I was not happy with the travel agent and made sure they knew about it.

I came back again in 2013 with my daughter, Meredith, in tow to ride around the course with me. This time everything was right, and I had a new set of Taylor Made clubs waiting for me. It was fall, and the course was in great shape. The 14th hole is a par 4 of 354 yards and is up the slope with a dog-leg to the right. Fairway bunkers on the right are well placed for an accurate tee shot. There are also three well-placed bunkers guarding the green on the right. Fairways are pretty narrow on most of the holes, and the 14th is no exception. I still think that golf in Italy is so relaxing and therapeutic that I have always played well here. I made my par here but struggled to shoot 75 despite the course length of just about 6,000 yards. I was proud that I was able to order my lunch in Italian, which capped off a perfect fall day in Tuscany.

NO. 15—PORTMARNOCK GOLF CLUB, DUBLIN, IRELAND

I am fortunate to be able to play Portmarnock every year on my annual business trip to Dublin, Ireland. Every time I play here, I have to take a photograph on the 15th tee, even though I have plenty of photographs of the hole. The quiet on this tee box is deafening and gets you focused on the task ahead. The 15th tee settles a few yards from the beach bordering the sea. The hole is one of the best par-3's in the world and one of the most scenic. The hole is daunting, since any shot lost on the right will end on the beach below. The hole measures out at 190 yards and 3 bunkers in the front of the ground will devour any tee shot that is short or doesn't carry the bunkers sufficiently so the shot can roll back into one of those bunkers. The green is fairly large for a par 3, so the tee shot must at least get to the middle of the green for a possible birdie. Any shot that is long to the back of the green has a risk of becoming a 3-putt affair. There is a swale just off the right of the green, which runs away from the hole. Chipping from the swale is not easy to stop the ball. Club selection is critical. You really need anything from a 3 iron to a hybrid club Wind will also come into play, so I wouldn't advise the hybrid club—something like the 4 or 5 iron will have to be hit well to carry the ball up to the green. Perhaps I've played Portmarnock too many times, but I believe it one of the most enjoyable venues that you could ever play—tough but fair throughout, and the 15th is its shining example of the best experience in links golf.

No. 15—TPC River Highlands, Cromwell, Connecticut

The 15th hole at TPC River Highlands is the beginning of a unique set of finishing holes that will test all aspects of your game. The course is home to the annual PGA Tour event, the Travelers' Championship. Most, if not all, the professionals will attempt to drive the 278-yard par 4 and try to make eagle or birdie to pick up a shot on the chase to the finish. The hole is certainly a "risk/reward" situation, as there are a number of hazards on the hole, including bunkers and the pond on the right extending to the back of the green. The professionals do make a bunch of birdies during the tournament. For the rest of us mere mortals, a hybrid club off the tee that finds the fairway will present a birdie opportunity as well. Risk/reward holes are fun to play, since it's possible to approach the holes with different types of strategies.

No. 16—Cape Kidnappers Golf Course, Hawkes Bay, New Zealand

The 16th hole at Cape Kidnappers is a 480-yard par 5 with a spectacular view of Hawkes Bay at the outermost part of the golf course. The preceding 15th hole is another par 5, which takes you to the end of the bay on a very steep ridge, which actually tilts forward into the ridge. You climb up to the 16th tee, which overlooks the 15th green from a series of well-placed wooden planks and gets to the tee box. The first thing to do is to take out a ball and knock it into Hawkes Bay from the elevated tee. The drop from the tee box into the bay is so steep that it will take 10 seconds for the ball to drop into the bay. Back to the golf game: the fairway is generous, and this hole has remarkable beauty. There are nine bunkers on the hole to be avoided, and the tee shot should be on the right side of the fairway to present an angle to get onto the green in regulation (3 shots). There isn't a lot of trouble here as long as you make the fairway, and a tee shot of 230 yards to the right side of the fairway will present a second shot that can be hit with a fairway wood for an easy chip shot of less than 100 yards. "Widows Walk" is just another one of Kidnappers' gorgeous holes where par should be more than possible.

No. 17—Plantation Course, Kapalua, Hawaii

The 17th hole at the Plantation Course in Kapalua, Hawaii is a 428-yard par 4. The key to this hole, unfortunately for most of us, is the length of the drive. The fairway is generous for the tee shot, but the positioning of the tee shot in the fairway is all-important. The fairway runs out 260 yards in the center of the fairway. Trees and jungle must be crossed at this point to reach the green. There is a smidge of fairway to the right, which could shorten the hole, but it would require a very precise drive of over 300 yards. Professionals hit 3 woods to the end of the fairway, where they then have an 8 iron to the large green that slopes from front to back. The second shot to the green is all carry, at least from the optimum spot in the fairway. If the drive is 230 yards or less, the shot directly to the green is 200 yards and almost all carry over the thicket of brush and jungle. From this position, the safe place is to carry the gorge with a shot that will land to the right of the green, leaving a pitch shot between 35-50 yards. This is an easy hole for the professionals but a daunting one for the amateur.

No. 18—Old Course at Saint Andrews

The 18th at St. Andrews is probably my favorite golf hole and one that I would like to play every day. It is the easiest hole on the course and follows the most difficult hole perhaps in all of golf–the 17th, known as The Road Hole. The 18th is a short 342- yard par 4 with the widest fairway in all of golf. The fairway is huge, since it is shared with the fairway on No. 1, so you actually have two fairways. Anyone who misses the fairway had better lie about missing it, since it is an embarrassment. When there is little to no wind, its possible to get pretty close to the green, and most of the professionals can drive the hole. The hole is also noted for the "Valley of Sin," which will punish any approach shot that is short and make getting up and down for par very difficult. It's a dramatic ending to an iconic setting, as you approach the green right in the middle of town as spectators line the fence on the right of the hole. You actually have a gallery as you come in and drink in the experience with all the history of this place. It is a wonderful experience for any golfer, irrespective of handicap, finishing the round of a lifetime.

No. 18—The Old Course at Half Moon Bay

The Old Course at Half Moon Bay was constructed as part of a real estate development project in the 1970s. For those readers who live outside of California, Half Moon Bay is a famous town on the Northern California coastline. Half Moon Bay is situated about 25 miles from San Francisco and 50 miles from Santa Cruz with a microclimate that keeps temperatures in the 50s and 60s throughout the year. You have to love fog and coolness to live here, as sunshine comes at a premium. Half Moon Bay's Maverick Beach boasts some of the greatest surf in the world and hosts many professional surf events. It is a mecca for surfers, with participants from all over the world. At the end of October, the town hosts the annual Pumpkin Festival, which draws hundreds of thousands of people and many kids for the ultimate pre-Halloween party. The area is also famous for its Christmas tree farms, and the post-Thanksgiving procurement of real Christmas trees gives the town another significant economic boost. So we have Mavericks, pumpkins, and Christmas trees—but what about golf?

The Old Course at Half Moon Bay used to be called Half Moon Bay Golf Course, with a combination of private golf membership with the public allowed to play as well. A number of years later, a Ritz Carlton hotel was constructed on the adjacent property to the Colony Beach Club, and a golf course was built there called the Ocean Course. The name of the course was then changed to the Old Course at Half Moon Bay to differentiate it from the new Ritz Carlton Ocean Course. The Old Course is inland in the Colony Beach community, but the final two holes finish at the Pacific Ocean. The 18th hole on the Old Course is a great way to finish what is a pretty nice golf course. The Pacific Ocean is the right boundary on the 18th hole and runs all of the 345 yards from tee to green. Weather conditions always come into play on the hole, with the potential for wind, fog, and at times rain, which complicate club selection. The hole's distinction is the crevice in the fairway about 190 yards from the tee. You could hit almost any club in your bag from 5 iron to 3 wood. A driver is likely to find the crevice, and your new Titleist will become yet another sacrifice to the Pacific Ocean below. It will take an accurate drive of 250 yards to carry the crevice. Most players will be intimidated by that choice, and so the idea will be to hit the tee shot as close to the crevice as possible, leaving an iron shot between 140-175 yards. The fairway is relatively generous, but position on the fairway is very important. The drive has to be in the middle of the fairway or slightly middle left to have a shot to the green that might yield a birdie putt. The fairway is generous but any shot hit too far to the left will leave a long approach shot to the green. The hole narrows significantly from the middle of the fairway and the Pacific looks even more menacing for the approach shot—there is no room to miss to the right, as there is nothing but rocks and the Pacific. The green is very large vertically and multi-tiered. On most days, the pin is placed in the front of the green to give the player a reasonable opportunity to make a birdie or a par. If the pin is placed on the top tier, any approach shot to the pin must be accurate and on line, or else the opportunity for disaster is magnified. Wind conditions make club selection difficult and really dictate how interesting the hole can be. It's a great finish to a very interesting golf course.

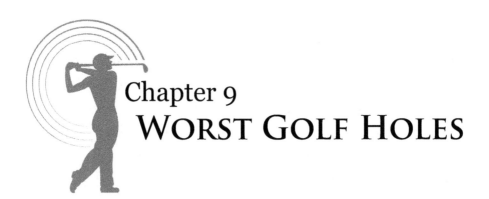

Chapter 9
WORST GOLF HOLES

I can't resist documenting some of the holes that blight an otherwise top global course. If I were a famous author, I would probably get some "hate" mail on these holes, but many players would agree with my assessment.

THE 18ᵀᴴ HOLE AT CYPRESS POINT CLUB IN MONTEREY, CALIFORNIA.

Cypress Point is the cathedral at the Monterey Peninsula. It is a privilege to play there, and the course consistently ranks in the top 5 of the US top 100 courses. You've played perhaps the finest 17 holes ever, and then you come to 18. You wonder if the architect ran out of ideas or real estate or both. The hole is a 380-yard par 4 with a grove of very large trees (cypress) right in the middle of the fairway. A tee shot of 220-230 yards is absolutely required, or these trees will encumber most second shots. From the tee box, it seems to be very difficult to pull this off. If you are able to execute the tee shot, you then face an uphill iron shot of 150-160 yards, which will play even longer due to the elevation from fairway to green. This hole is usually a double bogey for me, but the last time I played there, I hit a career tee shot of 280 yards that eluded the tree grove, giving me a 9 iron to the green. The hole is visually unattractive and is a poor closing hole to one of the best courses on the planet.

18th Hole on the Shore Course at Monterey Peninsula Golf Club

If I didn't know any better, I might think that the same person designed the 18th at Shore MPCC that designed the 18th at Cypress. Again, you've played 17 magnificent golf holes on the Shore Course, and now you've arrived on the 18th tee. It doesn't matter what tee box you play from front to back—the hole is a par 4 of anywhere from 360 yards to 385 yards. The problem here is not the hazards but the angle of the hole from tee to green. The hole is not quite a dogleg from right to left, but I might guess that it is a 150-degree turn. There is a huge bunker on the right that will catch any tee shot that is less than 200 yards, and it takes a power fade of 250 yards to clear the bunker and make the fairway. Any miss to the right of that bunker will result in a lost ball, impossible lie, or both. The player with a draw may have to contend with the bunker on the left side of the fairway. A tee shot of 230 yards or more that lands in the fairway could end up in this bunker. The second shot to the green is elevated, making club selection difficult. Severe bunkering on all sides protects the green, and any shots missed beyond those bunkers will result in impossible pitch shots. The green is very large despite the bunkering, and there is a mound about 15 paces onto the green which must be covered, or the ball will roll off the green, requiring a pitch shot to cover the mound. The hole is more difficult than the 18th at Cypress, but the angles make it visually very difficult to make par. While one can argue that the hole is challenging, some subtle redesign of the angles into the hole would remove this hole from the "worst" list.

THE 7TH HOLE AT PASATIEMPO GOLF CLUB

The 7th at Pasatiempo seems to be an afterthought, and I don't recall a hole like this one at another Alistair McKenzie design. The hole is a very short par 4 of 320 yards, and the fairway can't be more than 20 yards wide. The player has a number of options off the tee for club selection, from irons to driver. The ball must be in the fairway to make par or better. The hole opens up after the tree grove to a large green surrounded by excellent bunkering. A good tee shot will also require an accurate iron shot that must just clear the front bunker to get anywhere near the hole. The player who hits a high-trajectory ball should be able to hold the green, making par or birdie a possibility. The hole is visually sort of ugly, and there is nothing like it on the rest of this great course. The hole is impossible to redesign without felling some of the trees, and that's not a very good idea either.

4TH HOLE AT BOULDER RIDGE CC., SAN JOSE, CALIFORNIA

The fourth hole at Boulder is a par 4 of 410 yards. It has almost all the design flaws of any golf hole combined into one hole. The first point is that the tee shot is blind, which hurts both the good player and poor player. The fairway is straight away, but it has two levels. The good player could drive the ball through the fairway into a steep downhill lie. Stopping there, the poor player may not be able to drive the ball to the second level, living a shot of over 200 yards. The second shot is straight downhill approximately at a ten o'clock position to a massive green with large patches of rough on the left. The center and right sides of the hole are a sea of rough grass that slants away to the right. Any shot hit to the right of this hole will most certainly result in a double bogey or worse, which is far too penal for any golf hole. The high-handicapper has no choice and has to hit the ball to the left, hoping to avoid the huge bunker that protrudes from left to right. It is a huge bunker that is difficult to extricate to any decent position on the green. The design features of blind tee shot, blind end of the fairway, limited range to hit an approach shot to the green, and huge bunkering make this hole extremely unpleasant. I would characterize the hole as unpleasant and unfair, as opposed to a challenge for both good and poor player alike.

The 18th Hole at Spanish Bay Golf Links, Pebble Beach, California

Similar to the 18th hole at Cypress Point and the Shore Course at Monterey Peninsula Country Club, you have played 17 wonderful golf holes at then you reach the 18th hole. This hole is the worst design I have ever experienced on a golf course. I simply don't know what the designer was thinking to finish this wonderful golf course. The hole is a par 5 of 490 yards. The player generally has no clue where to hit to the tee shot. As you stand on the tee, there is a huge area of protected rough and trees on the left, which cannot be carried. Any tee shot in the fairway on the left is essentially a penalty shot despite being in the fairway. The tee shot must be on the right side of the fairway in order to have any opportunity to position the second shot. The right side of the fairway is actually no bargain either, as any shot that is missed slightly could end up in gorse or sea plants, and some shots might actually find the concrete cart path, leading to a fatal trip to the gorse. If the tee shot is perfect, you can hit anything from a wood to a long iron to get to the end of the fairway and hit it long enough to keep the left side of the hole out of play. The hole is essentially a very poor dogleg. The approach shot requires an accurate shot of 120-150 yards, depending on your position, over another sea of gorse and weeds with bunkers guarding the green. The green is huge but is horizontal in shape, so any shot that lands near the pin will probably run off the green to another horrible patch of environmentally sensitive area of gorse and weeds. Pin-seeking on this hole usually leads to some sort of disaster—either a 60-foot putt or a virtually impossible pitch from behind the green. The hole reminds me of the 4th hole at Pebble Beach in shape and direction, but the 4th at Pebble is a true and fair dogleg and the player is offered multiple options to reach the par 4 in two shots. The 18th at Spanish Bay offers no solace, as good shots are not rewarded and can be extremely punitive. A par on this hole is a minor miracle and a terrible ending to a well-designed golf course. Except for this hole, the designer did a great job developing a golf course through a piece of marsh and wetlands that offers a wonderful experience. I would scrap the dogleg and turn this hole into a challenging par 4 by eliminating the dogleg approach and building a proper green to end the round. It is usually a hole where players need at least 20 minutes to play the hole, or worse, with all the obstacles, potential bad bounces and horrible placement of the green. I don't think my opinion is a minority view among those players who have experienced this travesty.

9TH HOLE—STANFORD UNIVERSITY GOLF COURSE

Stanford is a great golf course, but the ninth seems to me to be a designer afterthought. The hole is a short par 4 of about 340 yards. It seems to me that the fairway is about 5 yards wide, which is ridiculous. The left side of the fairway is dotted with trees, some of which hang over the fairway, and the tee shot must carry all of these trees. The fairway is extremely narrow, with a funnel effect, and then widens, but the rest of the hole is significantly elevated. A good tee shot in the fairway at the 160-yard mark will actually play 180 yards or more to reach the green. The hole is a nightmare for a slicer, as the there is no opening on the right side, and the tree line is actually out of bounds. The slicer has no chance on this hole and will make a big number. The left side also is marked by a large bunker, which will cost you a full shot, since the second shot from the bunker will be entirely up hill. The hole is visually ugly from my point of view and detracts from the beauty of the preceding eight holes. Fortunately, this is the worst of the Stanford Golf Course, as the rest of the way in from 9 is very challenging and entertaining.

Chapter 10
IRELAND

I've been coming to Ireland for a long time for business and mostly for golf over the years. My first trip was in May 1982, when we played in the South Ballybunion, New Ballybunion, La Hinch, Waterville, and Tralee. Sadly, on that trip, we didn't see much of any of these courses, as we were pelted with wind, rain and fog. At La Hinch, we teed off in pouring rain and were thinking about coming in. Fortunately, the course layout escorts you back to the clubhouse from No. 1 to No. 4. When we saw local players beginning to tee off on No. 1 after we had completed the 4th hole, we knew that it was okay to proceed, as a number of locals had shown up after a Catholic Mass to begin their round. Many golfers believe that the golf course is the best way to communicate with the Lord, and our group could be counted in that crowd. After that first trip, almost every trip thereafter has been brilliant, with sunshine and little to no rain. In 2017, our luck ran out and we came up very short on the weather. Three rounds were played, and the weather played havoc with us in varying degrees in all of those rounds.

OLD HEAD

The club and the course are spectacular. My playing partner kept wishing that the weather would be good, as our round there was proceeded by business in The Netherlands. He kept looking at the Weather Channel on the net and was convinced that Old Head's microclimate would insulate us from significant trouble. What he didn't know was that the day before we were to play there, the club had to close the course due to horizontal rain and very high winds. His entreaties were not answered, as the wind was howling over 50 miles per hour. The course had been closed only one time before, so we were in for a real challenge. The club made us feel very welcome, and the guest suites are very well appointed and comfortable. What I especially liked was that my room faced the sea, with the lighthouse in full view outside of my door. The wind was howling, and that night I would sleep peacefully with the sliding glass door half open and the breeze completely filling the room as I dove under the covers.

I picked out a rental set of Titleist clubs and headed to the range for a quick warm-up. This was not the day to be hitting lofted clubs. Unfortunately, 3 irons and 4 irons are usually not included in rental sets, so we would be hitting a lot of 5 irons this day to keep the ball out of the wind. We played the front nine without a drop of rain, but the wind was blowing 40 miles per hour in all directions. It was only a matter of time before the heavens would begin the deluge. We proceeded to the treacherous, par 4, 12th hole and bam—here comes the rain-the grips on the clubs were gone in less than a minute (a record in my experience). Rain gloves and rain gear had to come on immediately and visibility was significantly reduced. It was very hard from there on and a tremendous "grind." You have to trust your swing and really focus to avoid caving in to the elements. It seemed like it took forever to play through 16 but we survived it. The 16th hole is a par 3 of 165 yards with the ocean on the right. The wind was blowing so hard that you had to aim your tee shot into the ocean and let the wind take it to the hole. The wind and rain were so hard that I had hit a driver to try to reach the green—I ended up coming up short but at least found dry land. Despite the weather, it was a wonderful experience and a good excuse for a return.

ROYAL DUBLIN

We left Old Head in great spirits and headed north to Dublin for a three-hour drive on a Friday afternoon. I had played Royal Dublin many years ago and hadn't remembered much about the course, as we played it in the middle of summer. Unfortunately, we had no practice time, and we ran up to the 1st tee with another set of Titlist rental clubs (again without a 3 iron or a 4 iron). Our sponsoring guest told us that we would be playing downwind for the front nine and directly into the wind for the back nine. The course was a lush green carpet of fairway and the greens were in perfect condition. I proceeded to rush through my opening tee shot and almost lost it as I hit it into the high heather on the right. I was very disappointed not to be able to take advantage of the downwind condition. I hate to rush to the first tee without any warm-up; I need to hit a few shots to find the tempo of the swing I'm bringing to the round. I managed to recover from there and persevere, but it seemed that every shot was getting a bad bounce, which disabled my ability to take advantage of the downwind conditions. We had spells of intermittent and high winds throughout the front nine. The conditions were tough but did not require the rain gear or the rain gloves. We reached the 456-yard par 4 with a drive and a 6 iron—not possible for me in normal conditions. My game would start to come together as we headed into the wind. All of a sudden, drives were straight down the middle, with good length, and pars started to happen in rapid fashion.

The highlight of the round occurred on the par-5 18th hole that I had completely forgotten about. I thought this was an easy hole from my past memory, but I was mistaken. I drove the ball off the tee with a 3 wood right down the middle to the end of the fairway, avoiding the first burn that would require a carry of 270 yards. Erroneously, I thought another 3 wood would carry the second burn onto the huge green, as large as the greens at St. Andrews. I thought at the time it was a par 4. The second shot would have to carry 215 yards to clear the burn and catch the green. Between the second shot and the greenside burn is a tangled mess of high rough and mayhem. It seemed like a gigantic mess of salad greens. I felt very good about the shot and pulled a 3 wood and carried everything, landing the ball about 80 feet from the hole (that's how big the green is). As I walked up to the green to see where the shot was, I was amazed at what I had accomplished—that was not the way to play the hole. Anything short of the green would have landed in the spinach or the burn, and a big number would have been recorded. Of course, my eagle putt was 20 feet short in the conditions, and I settled for a par 5. Christy O'Connor, Jr., the famous Irish professional, would play this hole with a 4 iron down the left side of the fairway and then hit another 4 iron to clear the second burn to be within chipping distance of the green. I played the hole incorrectly but still escaped with a par.

ROYAL PORT MARNOCK

I've played Port Marnock every year for the past five years, and it's a course you would like to play every day and never tire of it. It seems that times were becoming prosperous for Port Marnock, as I noted some capital improvements around the course and the infrastructure of the club. The wind would howl again but not as badly as our experience at Old Head or Royal Dublin. It was as if the Irish gods were smiling, stating, "You've endured enough, so we'll just give you a taste of the wind and the rain." The worst of the weather came on holes 13-15, where the rain pelted down on us, but not badly enough to kill the grips on the clubs. I had the audacity to leave my rain gloves at the hotel, presuming that we would have decent weather. I was almost incorrect in this assessment, as my rain gloves after the round at Old Head took two days to dry out. Unlike Royal Dublin, the winds at Port Marnock can come from all sides, so you have to be careful with aim and direction, making club selection difficult at times. The course is always challenging, but I hit every fairway with the driver and scored pretty well, which made the round very enjoyable.

The scenic par 3 is right on the ocean, as the prevailing wind was blowing left to right towards the ocean. The hole played to its yardage of 164 yards, and I chose a 6 iron to fade into the green—my shot landed on the green but fell off slightly to the right. The pin was on a crown on the green, and the wind pushed the shot off the green but only about 5 feet, making for a relatively easy pitch shot for a par. Our group played well the entire day, as it got pretty dark on the 17th hole on this gray dull day. The 18th hole is a wonderful finishing hole, with an elevated green requiring a short iron past the pin, as anything short of the pin would fall off the green by at least 20 yards. It was another terrific day at Port Marnock with a bit more of a weather challenge, as October weather in Ireland is rather unpredictable. Of course, the next day was sunny and mild, and I'm sure Dublin's Chamber of Commerce was out taking pictures for the vacation brochures.

The K Club—Irish Golf Experience

The Kildare Hotel, Spa & Country Club ("K" Club) is located about 20 miles outside of Dublin, Ireland. The Club is highly rated, and the golf course has been a venue for the Ryder Cup in 2006. We eagerly awaited getting there after playing extensively in Dublin over the previous week. Unfortunately, the weather was unseasonably warm for Ireland in August as we rolled up to the hotel in our fabulous Skoda. Most guests who come to the K Club arrive in a Ferrari, Bentley, Porsche, Jaguar, etc. We arrived triumphantly with our rented Skoda. I was still fuming at the arrangements that were made by the Irish golf tour booking company. As an aside to this experience, never, ever book a golf tour with a booking service in the Republic of Ireland, Scotland, England or anywhere else. It is a total rip-off, and I'm still upset about this one after five years.

The hotel was fabulous and well appointed. We looked forward to our dinner as we arrived in late afternoon. It was Friday and we would be playing Saturday and then returning to Dublin, so we only had one night here. The meal at the club was supposed to be part of our tour package but, alas, the vouchers the touring company gave us for dinner covered only about 40% of the total cost. We had a late tee time on Saturday at 2:00 p.m. on the championship course. I had been having some trouble with my left knee with all the walking we had been doing in the previous week, so I needed a golf cart to get around. The fun started when we entered the pro shop. It seemed that the staff greeted us with a bit of indifference. For a minute, I thought I was at Royal Liverpool in England. I told them I would need a golf cart and they started to make excuses that they didn't have any available—key word, available. There were carts everywhere, so when I asked about that, there was no answer. I told them I wouldn't be able to play without a cart and so, reluctantly, they produced one.

We had arrived early to purchase some logo merchandise, and it was about noon and we decided to loosen up and hit some balls. We were told that the range was closed to non-members until 1p.m. I was flabbergasted, as there was plenty of room on the range to accommodate the entire tee sheet for the afternoon. I couldn't believe it—an English experience in Ireland—it had never happened before, but I guess there is time and place for everything. The last straw came when we went to the first tee to join our playing partners, who were drawn to play with us. One of the players was an American in the golf business and the other was a businessman from Poland. The starter looked with disdain at the Polish businessman who was wearing "cargo shorts." The starter stared at him for a few minutes and then stated, "You can't play the course with those shorts; those type of shorts are expressly prohibited on this course as part of our rules."

The Polish businessman stated that no one had explained this rule and was happy to take his money to play the course. He said, "I don't have any other clothes, and I'm not staying here. I would have to go back to Dublin to change my clothes." After considerable discussion and negotiation with the starter, we were finally able to tee off and begin the round.

The course was disappointing to me after all the courses we had played in Dublin. In previous years, we had played some of the great courses in the south of the country such as Waterville, Tralee, Ballybunion. Although those courses are links venues, this parkland didn't measure up for me. I was especially unhappy with the 17th hole, as my 5-iron approach shot hit the green 20 feet to the right of the hole only to spin 45 feet from right to left off the green and into the water hazard. The green wasn't even tilted—it was pretty flat, so I still can't account for how this could have occurred.

We left the K Club with an unsavory taste in our mouths, without a yen to return anytime soon.

Another Irish Experience— Old Head Golf Links, Kinsale, Ireland

The experience we had at Old Head Golf Links was entirely the opposite of the K Club experience. Old Head is located in the south of Ireland near Cork, in the town of Kinsale. The course itself is a remarkable tract of land of over 200 acres on a peninsula adjoining the Atlantic Ocean. A view from the air gives you the idea that this is an impossible tract for a golf course. The operation of the club is very efficient, and we received a genuine Irish warm welcome. The club boasts a series of suite rooms for its guests that are cozy, comfortable, and well appointed. We were concerned about the weather, and our apprehension would prove to be appropriate as the day wore own. The club had to close the course the day before in wind and torrential rain that made play impossible. It was blowing hard again, but rain was forecast for later in the day. We had a 1 p.m. tee time, so it was going to be close. Little did we know that it would be closer than we thought.

The first hole was a pleasant opening of 390 yards as a par 4, and it seems to be a welcoming statement that says, "This is not so difficult." That feeling is over as you step into the 2nd tee box, another par 4 of 376 yards, and see the intimidating tee shot. The ocean must be crossed on the left side and is in play, so the tee shot must be hit to the right side of the fairway. The wind was blowing hard toward the ocean, so the tee shot had to be aimed way right. The 3rd hole is an absolutely beautiful par 3 with the cliffs on the left to catch any tee shot that aims for the flagstick. The ball must be hit to the right and let the wind take care of the rest. Yardages are relatively meaningless for club selection on these types of holes when the wind is howling and moving the ball from right to left. I don't like to like to hit the ball high in the air in these conditions, and unfortunately, we didn't have a 4 iron in the rental set, so a 5 iron had to be hit. The 4th hole is a 423-yard par 4 with another carry required down the right side of the hole. Wind made it impossible to get home in two, but we got close enough to get up and down for a par. On we went through the par 5's and the rest of the front nine. The wind was howling, but we were still dry. We were really enjoying this venue, despite the wind that was blowing nearly 40 mph.

Then we got to the 12th hole, which is probably the most difficult hole on the course. We played it as a par 5 of 537 holes. The tee shot was blind and had to be hit way right to reach the fairway. Any shot hit to the middle or left would find rocks and the ocean below. The heavens opened and in a matter of 30 seconds, the rain came down violently and horizontal. I decided to wait a few minutes and not put on the rain pants, which turned out to be a big mistake. By time I was ready to hit my third shot into the green, I was soaked and had to don the rain pants. The club grips were gone, and fortunately I had brought rain gloves with me. Rain gloves work only when wet and provide an adhesive that allows the player to grip the club almost normally. There was no way to hit this green, as the wind was ferocious and howling to over 50 mph. These conditions were the worst I had played in since a similar round at the Old Course at St. Andrews. These conditions were actually worse, since the wind was blowing harder. I kept hitting 5 irons to keep the ball in the middle to spots I could chip from, so I made a very satisfying par here in these conditions. In conditions like these, you really have to focus on your swing mechanics and discipline to avoid succumbing to the conditions. These types of conditions never bother the professionals, since they have the ability to keep that focus and execute their routines. If this had been a professional tournament, play would have been suspended.

Nevertheless, we soldiered on and were actually playing better through focus and perseverance, with encouragement from our caddies. We reached the par-3 16th hole of 176 yards, with the wind blowing hard from the ocean on the right to the left. You had to bring yourself to the idea that you had to aim the tee shot into the ocean on the right and let the wind carry it to the left and hopefully on the green. The wind was blowing so hard and the rain was teeming so I could no longer play with my eyeglasses and had to remove them. I decided to hit driver into this wind and aimed the ball over the Atlantic. It fell short of the green but between the two greenside bunkers. We trudged through the last two holes quite proud of the accomplishment of finishing. Many people had walked off as the conditions continued to deteriorate.

Despite the conditions, it was a marvelous experience, and I hope I have the opportunity to do it again. The entire Old Head experience was wonderful, and the Irish hospitality was first-rate. It was a far cry from the experience at the K Club.

Chapter 11
EXPERIENCES

CURING THE SLICE

The slice is one of the most common faults that plague the high-handicap player. The slice can result from different faults with the swing, which are impossible to document in a book like this one. Besides, I would be the least qualified to give golf lessons to anyone, as I'm still taking them myself after all these years. Despite all this, I believe I can fix the slice of a high-handicap player. The slice results basically when the clubface is "open" when the ball is struck.

During a competitive golf match at our club, my opponent kept slicing the ball off the tee all day long, and despite the number of strokes I had to give him, I was able to win the match pretty handily. After the round, I told him that could cure his slice in five minutes or less. He looked at me as if I were from the planet Mars. "Yep, I can fix your slice and I can fix it in five minutes or less, "I said. "Meet me up at the driving range in a few minutes, and we'll get this done." He looked at me rather skeptically but decided that he would go for the cure.

We arrived at the driving range, and I told him that I only had one condition: he had to swing exactly the way he had been hitting the ball all day. Of course, he agreed—I approached and changed his ball alignment and stance ever so slightly. I could tell that his swing and stance were producing an exaggerated move that opened his clubface at impact, forcing the ball to the right—in many cases way right. I didn't and couldn't fix his swing mechanics, as that is the job of the golf professional. I essentially moved him into a position with his swing where the clubface would be square at impact irrespective of his swing mechanics.

He took this new stance and swung, and the ball came off the clubface straight as a string, right down the middle. He turned and looked at me and said, "That was luck. It'll never happen again." I told him to hit another ball—and click, the ball went straight down the middle again. He was blown away and hit fifteen more balls right down the middle. I told him, "You're cured, but if you change your swing, all bets are off." I now have a free meal waiting for me at the restaurant he owns in town.

THE 2016 RYDER CUP

In *Golf Chronicles*, I had covered a few of the cups and cited that the event was becoming non-competitive. I also criticized that the event was becoming a jingoistic nightmare, with fans screaming and taunting competitors, even to the point of booing bad shots. The European team has won 8 of the last 10, and supposedly the US effort was in disarray. I believed that the event was at risk of becoming irrelevant, as it seemed that there was very little media coverage of the 2016 Cup at Hazeltine, CC in Minnesota leading up to the event.

All of this has been proven to be incorrect. The European team continued to focus on their winning formula under captain Darren Clarke. Clarke has had a lot of success in participating in this event and knows how to win. The team was anchored by a very hot Rory McElroy, who had just won the Fed Ex Cup the week before in spectacular fashion. The team also featured Open Championship winner, Henrik Stenson, and a number of new very good European players who would be experiencing Ryder Cup play for the first time.

The PGA of America had decided after the dismal showing in the last Cup that something would have to change. A task force was set up to make the necessary changes to produce a competitive team that could play together. The US side has been criticized as a group of elitist millionaires who didn't need to be told what to do or how to behave as a team. The US selected Davis Love, a proven winner and good communicator, to be the captain of the team. The US side also added a number of winning advisors such as Tiger Woods, Jim Furyk, and others. The stars, such as Jordan Speith, anchored the team; Patrick Reed complemented with veterans such as Brandt Snedeker and Phil Mickelsen.

The stage was set, and the matches commenced. The fan noise was raucous and actually outrageous. The amazing part of this event, which I've never seen before, was that the energy of the fans actually transferred to the players. The PGA runs ads for its weekly events, showing great shots with the tag line, "These Guys are Good." Well, in this event, those ads will have enough material for the foreseeable future. I have never seen so many remarkable shots in any event in my memory. A great example was the first match of the Singles on Sunday in a match between Rory McElroy and Patrick Reed. McElroy reached the par-4 7th hole but had a 75-foot putt for birdie. Patrick was pin high but some 35 feet away. The fans taunted McElroy, citing Reed's advantage. It seemed that both players would two-putt this hole and walk away, halving it with pars. McElroy had a potential risk of a three-putt, given the length of this putt. McElroy stared down this incredible long putt and holed it, and went berserk with emotion, gesturing to the fans that were still jeering him. McElroy covered his ears and beckoned to the crowd, "I can't hear you." Reed had performed this similar taunt in the 2014 Cup at Gleneagles to the screaming European contingent. Reed would have to hole the 35-footer to halve the hole. It's a putt that you would never think about holing, but Reed did just that; the crowd erupted in glee, and Reed did a rain dance on the green. What was significantly different this time, and in this Ryder Cup, is that Reed went up to McElroy and gave him a fist pump, admiring what he had just accomplished. Both players congratulated each other and moved to the next hole. This type of behavior would never have occurred in prior Cups, as I believe the crowd is actually producing an adrenaline rush for these players, bringing out the best skills they have. In other events, these outbursts would be distracting and actually produce negative results with animosity for the players.

Seve Ballesteros would have loved this.

Trump Golf Links at Ferry Point

I couldn't resist, especially in the exciting election year 2016, playing Trump Golf Links at Ferry Point. In the usual hyperbole that accompanies anything associated with the Trump Organization, the website boasts that this course "will become the greatest public golf course and facility in New York City." Well, that's not saying much, because I can't recall any other public golf course within the New York City limits that's worth a lick.

The course is situated in the Bronx, just beneath the Whitestone Bridge, so the views of the Manhattan skyline and the Bridge are pretty cool. The links-style course is a nice design by Jack Nicklaus, and a good concept is the number of tee boxes where you can play the course from 6038 yards to 7407 yards. We decided to play the course from the short tees, since we had no knowledge of the place, and the course enabled me to hit short and medium irons to the greens. The course is well bunkered and perfectly placed to catch many tee shots. The bunkers on some holes require very accurate tee shots to avoid. The course was devoid of significant links-style rough—it was there, but it was cut down, probably to maintain pace of play. The course is a good challenge, especially from the gold tees at about 6900 yards, but the straight hitter will be rewarded more than the player who can crush 300-yard tee shots. I really liked the course design, mostly due to the strategic nature of the bunkering, as bunkers come into play on many of the holes, especially the par 3's. The greens are in terrific shape for a relatively new course and putted very true. I estimated the speed at about 10-11 on the stimp meter, which was good for the player who usually plays faster greens. The best hole was the par-5 18th hole of 527 yards, where we played from the blue tees. The fairway is generous enough, but a drive hit over the left fairway bunker gives the golfer a good angle for a second shot position. The hole seems to be the signature hole for the course, as you get a wonderful view of the Whitestone Bridge as you come in to complete your round. The front pin was in use on this day, so the approach shot brought the front bunkers into play. Like most links courses, the course could be made extremely difficult by allowing the golf fescue to grow to heights that you would experience in Scotland and Ireland. The rough in Scotland and Ireland is usually a stroke penalty, since you have to extricate yourself back into the fairway with a sand wedge or short iron.

When we completed the round, we went into the makeshift clubhouse for a 19th-hole libation. Trump states that they are building a $10M clubhouse eventually on the site, but I'm sure that will be dependent on how much New York City contributes to the effort (opinion only). The waiter came up to us to take our order, and my playing partner asked for a "Hillary Clinton." He was trying to make a joke, but the waiter gave a look that could kill. Needless to say, the service standard dropped quite a bit.

THE GOLF CLUB THROW

Most golfers associate the throwing of a club on the golf course as poor behavior at best. Golf played while angry is never any fun, and the throwing of a club is looked upon with utter disdain by playing partners.

I hadn't thrown a golf club in over twenty years, since I'm aware of what horrible behavior that it represents. If I became angry or emotional over a poor shot, I might slam a club into the ground, take a deep breath, and move on. I also don't do this very often—maybe once every five years or so. It also isn't very good behavior, but at least it is a one-or-two-second fit of temper that gets that bad shot out of your system, so you can recompose yourself and move on. I condone this type of behavior because I've seen many professionals do the same thing. Of course, I'm kidding myself, because it also demonstrates bad behavior and etiquette on the golf course.

My latest incident of the golf club thrown was very existential. I had hit my drive very well down the left side of the fairway of the 427-yard par 4 at Cordevalle Golf Club. The hole is a dogleg to the left, with a very large tree marking the dogleg. Any shot hit just further left would end up behind the tree, making it very difficult to make it to the green. The hole on the right has two bunkers—one bunker is about 75 yards from the hole, and the other bunker is a greenside bunker. I had just hit past the tree, but my ball landed in a little bit of rough and squirted out a bit into the fairway. The tree was not in the way, but I would have to hit the ball precisely to avoid the two bunkers. I had 185 yards to the hole, but my opening was no more than 3 yards, as any shot hit more than a yard from this opening to the right would end up in one of those bunkers. Any shot pulled to the left might make contact with a tree branch, so it was a pretty delicate shot. I selected a 4 iron, figuring that I had a chance to negotiate this 3-yard window and perhaps land the ball on the right side of the green to roll onto the green.

I took my stance and flushed the 4 iron. I was sure that I had accomplished my objective. I couldn't see the result, as the fairway rises and then goes down to the hole. My playing partner, who was fortunate to have a wider window and see the green from the fairway, reported the result of my shot. Bad luck—the ball hopped as I had planned but took a bad bounce to the right and was in the bunker. It was then that I had this wonderful conversation with my 4 iron. I didn't react with any emotion or anger, because I was so satisfied with the strike of the club, and I was really pleased as to the how the ball shot off the club. It was then that I had a conversation with the 4 iron. The club simply had to be thrown. The first point of conversation with the 4 iron was that the shot was terrific and both player and implement had executed the shot as planned. The second point was that I had to compliment the 4 iron, as our partnership has been particularly effective since I bought the club especially from Nakashima, the club design company in Stockton, California. The third point that I wanted to make with the 4 iron that I had no evil intentions, anger, or any other motive for the action I was about to take. The fourth point was that I told the 4 iron that I was going to throw it. The purpose of throwing it was not to express anger of my bad luck with the result of the shot, but to extricate any future demons that I might have with the club. After this conversation, I took the 4 iron and flung it in a helicopter like fashion about 20 yards down the fairway. I strolled down the fairway without any emotion and picked up the club, cradled it, and put it back in my bag. My playing partners said nothing, and the game went on.

I was now lying 2 in the fairway bunker 64 yards from the hole. This is a pretty long bunker shot, and in front of me was the greenside bunker. The flag position was directly over the greenside bunker, so the shot would have to be hit at least 70 yards to get close to the hole. I was pretty pessimistic as I approached this endeavor, and I decided to take a 56-degree wedge for the shot. I hit the shot high in the air and headed straight toward the flagstick. I anticipated a terrific result and waited as the ball came down, and then—boom—the ball hit the green and spun back into the greenside bunker.

My playing partners couldn't believe my poor luck, as they thought the shot was terrific. I didn't react with any emotion and climbed out of this bunker and headed for the next one—the greenside bunker. Of course, the ball had nestled in the bottom of the steep bunker, and I had no more than 10 feet of green to work with. I expressed no emotion as I approached taking my stance in the green side bunker. I proceeded to hit a terrific bunker shot and holed the shot for an improbable par 4. The conversation with the 4 iron, and the subsequent throwing of the 4 iron without anger and emotion enabled me to accept another one of golf's many quirks. It's something I may never do again, but it just felt right in these circumstances.

Chapter 12
INSTRUCTION

I can't resist about writing about instruction. As someone who has been playing the game for over forty years, I have formed some definite opinions about instruction that I don't think would be published anywhere.

Some tenets of instruction:

1. Instruction is relevant for all levels of player—from the professional to the amateur hacker.

2. There is unfortunately no single methodology of instruction that will improve your game at any level.

3. It is impossible for the amateur to succeed at emulating the capability of the professional.

4. Instruction is NOT reading golf publications and looking at and then trying to duplicate photography shown in those publications.

5. Claims and boasts of techniques that will promise additional yardage are claims that are equivalent to

buying pills and concoctions that promise weight reduction.

We've now described what is instruction is not—so just what is instruction?

Good instruction is having the PGA professional or equivalent credentialed teacher work with the amateur and build a swing for that student. There are many fine golf instructors, but instruction is a very personalized thing, almost equivalent to the relationship between doctor and patient. The player has to trust the instructor implicitly and cannot use multiple instructors. The player should not take instruction and then try to adapt the instruction to golf tips heralded in *Golf Digest*. None of this ever works.

Instruction is a bit like going to school. Depending on your skill and what you are trying to accomplish, you either enter elementary school, high school, college, or post-graduate school, depending on your handicap and your personal goals for the game. I have learned this lesson the hard way through multiple instruction attempts; I have now chosen one professional who works with me consistently. I don't take instruction advice from anyone else.

Everyone has a unique way of playing the game, including set-up, club grip pressure, stance, club head speed, etc. What I have had found to be successful is to take instruction in bites to form the foundation of the golf swing. Some bits or topics will come easier than others, and others will take a long time to develop and require consistent practice. As you learn and master something new, you always must practice what you've learned to maintain the foundation and continue to improve. The worst thing is to assume that your fundamentals are fine and discover new faults since you haven't practiced these fundamentals. In order to take advantage of the instruction, take notes and develop a "checklist" for every swing until the technique becomes so repetitive

THE PRO-AM ON THE PROFESSIONAL GOLF TOUR

The Pro-Am is a staple of the PGA Tour. It gives the amateur the opportunity to play a round of golf with the touring PGA professional. PGA tour players are required to play in this event, which, for most tournaments, is an 18-hole best ball event on the Wednesday with the professional and four amateur players. The Pro-Am is a key event for the PGA, as it is a fundraiser for the local charities that the tournament and the PGA support for the local community where the event is held. The format for the tournament is a best ball event, where double bogey is the highest score that can be recovered. This type of scoring gives the PGA the opportunity to complete the event in less than five hours, which the professionals truly appreciate. The professionals treat these events in various ways. They know they have to support the event and the amateurs to maintain their reputations and support the event that sponsors their livelihood. I found a wide variety of behaviors demonstrated by the professionals in many of these Pro-Am events, ranging from arrogance at its worst to graciousness at its best. In one event at the Shell Houston Open, the professional didn't say a word to us during the entire round. He will remain nameless here, but he was at one time the No. 1 Player in the world.

The amateur travels Sunday to the tournament site on Sunday for the Monday evening pairings party, when the amateur will be paired to his professional partner. It's the usual corporate affair, with and hob-nobbing through the crowd of corporate sponsors and guests. Tuesday is usually a practice round with the professional and your team, as you get ready for the Wednesday event.

I played in many of these types of events, primarily due to my position in my company and my good fortune to be the only senior executive who played golf in the company, so all the invites came to me. I've played in many events on the PGA Tour and the Senior PGA Tour. The Senior Tour events are more fun, because you get to play two rounds with your professional partner rather than just one as is the case with the PGA Tour.

My best experience was the Phoenix Open in 1995, which was a very special affair called the Charity Cup, sponsored by Motorola. Our company was one of Motorola Semiconductor's largest suppliers, so I was on the invitee list. What made this event special was that it was the same day as the Super Bowl. The Pro Am would start at 9 a.m. and finish by 12:30, and then we would be taken by helicopter (brand-new McDonnell Douglas models, which were for sale) with our spouses/significant others to attend the Super Bowl between the Dallas Cowboys and the Pittsburgh Steelers. We stayed at the Princess Hotel, which adjoins the Tournament Players Club of Scottsdale, where the tournament would be played. In January, days in Phoenix start off briskly with temperatures in the low 30s. We were on the driving range at 7:15 a.m., and it was a pretty amazing situation. I was warming up with Tom Watson on my right and Nick Faldo on my left. Each pairing in this Pro-Am would consist of one PGA Tour player and one professional football player. I was going to be playing with Dan Pohl and Dan Marino. The driving range was amazing, with all the PGA professionals and professional football players warming up at the same time. I remember Lanny Wadkins running up and down the line soliciting autographs from the football players.

We went to the first tee at the TPC venue and found the fairways lined with fans. My partner, a Motorola senior executive, dribbled his tee shot about 40 yards down the left side of the fairway. The crowd was immense, with many followers of Dan Marino wearing all types of Miami Dolphins paraphernalia. My knees were knocking as I witnessed this tee shot as I took my stance. I simply blotted that shot out of my memory and laced a drive right down the middle about 235 yards. I was pleased, as once the first tee shot was away, I would not be affected or distracted by the crowd. Due to the Super Bowl event that would start later that day, the Pro-Am was actually being televised by ESPN. I made it on television as I holed a 35-foot putt on the 14th hole for birdie, and Marino slapped me a high five as ESPN had it live. It was a terrific event and probably the only time that this event will occur in the same place as the Super Bowl. We were helicoptered to the Stadium for the Super Bowl, which was only a 25-minute ride, but I was a mess for that ride. I haven't been in a helicopter ever since.

I had played in so many of these events that the Senior Professional, Dale Douglass, asked me if I held a job or did I play in Pro-Ams for a living. Dale is a terrific guy, and I played in four senior Pro-Am events with him.

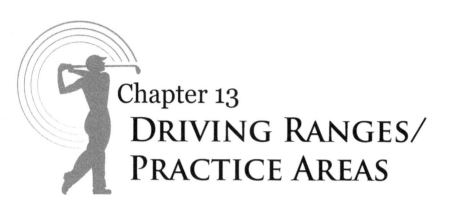

Chapter 13
DRIVING RANGES/ PRACTICE AREAS

Why would anyone want to write about driving ranges? In all the golf books in my library, I have yet to encounter a description of the driving range or practice area. There is significant amount of variability in what driving ranges look like all over the world, which would stupefy the average golfer.

The purpose of the driving range is basically twofold:

1. To warm up before your round golf and see what type of swing you are taking into your round.

2. To work on you're game and try to incorporate new techniques or fix some bad habits (at least temporarily).

Most of the effort spent on the driving range has to do with the second purpose, and this is where most of the time is spent.

Driving ranges vary from the pristine and most elegant venues to the ugliest and saddest facilities you have ever seen.

Private Club Ranges in the United States

The best private club range in the United States and the world is at the Monterey Peninsula Country Club in Pebble Beach, California. Point Joe was redesigned in 2016 concurrently with the redesign of the Dunes Course at MPCC. I don't think there is another driving range on the planet where you are driving balls toward the Pacific Ocean. The Pacific is actually a half-mile away, so you won't be driving balls into the ocean, but the views are spectacular, especially at sunset. The teeing ground is equivalent to the fairways at MPCC and always immaculate. The design of the range is unique, in that there are multiple flags at yardages from 50 yards to over 250 yards, surrounded by bunkers to give the player the opportunity to simulate playing an actual golf hole. All ranges have flags and yardages, but they have no shape, and the player has no feel for the accuracy and distance control required on the course. At Point Joe, you are actually hitting shots to greens, so you achieve the opportunity for distance and accuracy of your iron shots. The range is complemented by two practice putting greens and a bunker practice area that simulate the actual golf course. Point Joe rates as the best practice area I have ever experienced.

There are two other ranges worth noting. One is Pine Valley, where the course is so difficult you have to be prepared to hit a number of fairway bunker shots. This comment is probably an exaggeration, but there seems to be more sand on Pine Valley than fairway, so accuracy is very important. The practice facility at Pine Valley simulates course conditions very well. The other notable facility is at La Hontan, a private club in Truckee, California. La Hontan offers a range as well as a full 18-hole practice facility, which is pristine and challenging.

Many private clubs do not have the sufficient real estate or the topography to install good practice facilities. The worst type of range is one where you are hitting the ball uphill, so distance control is an illusion. For these ranges, all you can do is warm up and hope for the best when you start playing the course.

PUBLIC FACILITIES-UNITED STATES

The driving range can also be a place for social gathering and pure fun, and many public facilities offer food and beverage where players of all skill levels can whale away at the golf ball.

These ranges usually have no teeing ground and offer astro-turf like "mats" to hit balls, with rubber tees for your driving clubs. The "mats" give you a false sense of security, since the lie of the ball is always flat and perfect, so an average player will look like a professional at these facilities. The balls usually have half the compression of a normal ball but fly wonderfully off the "mats." Some ranges have multiple tiers to increase capacity of the facility to rake in more money. These facilities are great for those people who don't play the game very much or at all and just want to get out and have a good time. The purpose served here is basically fun, and you won't be improving your game in these facilities. There are certainly exceptions to developing your game, as Tiger Woods can attest to. He spent many a day at the public facility in his developmental years with his dad.

I do have a "beef" with many of these public facilities, which have signs all over the place telling what you can do or not do, which clutters the ambience of these venues. In these facilities, the operative term is "driving range," not "practice facility."

ENGLAND AND IRELAND

The English and the Irish have not adopted the concept of the driving range. There are some public facilities in the UK that operate in a similar fashion to the United States. Most private clubs in England and Ireland do not even have practice facilities. In some cases, there are patches of ground that are available for you to practice, provided you have the patience to bring your own practice balls and pick them up yourself. There is no practice facility at Port Marnock in Dublin, Ireland, so you tee it up at this wonderful venue with only the hope that you can duplicate your last good swing. The range at the K club in Ireland was a very weird, and they decided to limit the times that the guests of the hotel can actually use the range, so this restriction prohibited our ability to warm up at all. There was no range that I could find at the Old Course at St. Andrews, but there has to be a place where the professionals can practice, though I never saw it despite the number of times I played there.

JAPAN

The Japanese driving-range experience is a unique combination of ball striking, social gathering, and general good cheer. In Japan, golf is still a very expensive proposition, and for many players, it is the only opportunity that they will get to hit a golf ball. Many players will never see a Japanese golf course, and most of their play will come when they take a vacation in Hawaii or some other Asian destination. Golf driving ranges are everywhere in the country. The facilities are usually pristine, replete with mats and multiple tiers. The entire facility is netted such that the real estate requirement for a range is small and compact. The balls are dispensed by machine and there is no ball pickup required. The balls are automatically retrieved into an underground system where they collect and are funneled back into the machines. The underground system washes the balls, so they are returned to the machine in the same clean state that they were struck. The ranges tend to be no more than 225 yards in length so it's a lot of fun to try to hit some drivers though the netting and out of the range. The slots are usually covered, so you can hit balls rain or shine. It's not cheap, and a large bucket of balls will cost between $15-$20. There are no signs, and the civility and etiquette of the customers is to be revered. There is no club bashing or swearing, and you might feel that you're in a church. For some Japanese, golf is a religion even if they never see the golf course. There are virtually no driving ranges at the golf courses themselves, so your warm-up may be the night before you actually play. The driving range experience in Japan is a must, to appreciate the fervor and dedication of the Japanese player.

Chapter 14
MAJOR
CHAMPIONSHIPS

MASTERS TOURNAMENT

It's Master's Weekend-2017 and the first two rounds are complete with blustery windy conditions. The wind and the cold had a significant impact on the field, with fewer than ten contestants breaking par. This is the first Master's without the presence of Arnold Palmer; the opening first tee ceremony honored him, and there were enough tears to go around, including fellow legends Jack Nicklaus and Gary Player. It was a wonderful moment as Nicklaus, at age seventy-seven, blasted a tee shot down the first fairway perhaps besting fellow legend Gary Player (at age eighty-one) by a few yards. Arnold would have loved to see it.

The leaders in the clubhouse were Sergio Garcia and Charlie Hoffman. Hoffman hails from San Diego, and has a good Master's record. He had an amazing back nine, getting iron shots close to the holes for birdie opportunities on the back nine, shooting 65 in the opening round. He faltered a bit in the second round, with a 3 over 75, leaving him at 4 under par for the tournament tied with Garcia. Sergio had never won a major and had been very close many times. Perhaps this would be his first time. He struck the ball very well and made quite a few chips and putts around the treacherous greens, and there was hope that he could continue to do this for the last two rounds. His putter on day 4 had usually been his demise in major events.

The biggest surprise in the event was the difficulty of the par-5 15th hole, which the contestants believe is a birdie hole and also presents an eagle opportunity. The conditions for the first two days with wind and cold prevented the players from going for the green in two. Most of the players had between 240-260 yards to the green, as their tee shots were not running as they usually do in this generous fairway. In past years, contestants had driven the ball over 300 yards, leaving them iron shots for birdie and eagle opportunities. In the first two days, the pond that surrounded the front and backside of the green became a factor in these conditions. A shot that made the green but didn't carry far enough forward would spin back into the pond's watery grave. A shot that carried the green and went over the green faced a very difficult pitch back onto the green, which could result in three putts or worse. Jordan Speith, my favorite to win the tournament, discovered this problem on the first day when his shot to the green of 250 yards spun back into the pond. His penalty pitch shot flew the green, and he recorded a calamitous 9 for this hole. No player that has recorded a higher score on a hole than 7 has ever won a Master's, and this history would continue.

On the third day of the event, the players faced another different golf course. The wind was well down and not a factor, but the greens started to harden, and putting would be extremely difficult.

At the end of the day, Sergio Garcia emerged victorious and got the "not winning a major" monkey off his back. He slayed the dragon, beat back the demons, and any other trite expression that you can come up with. He won the championship in a dramatic playoff victory over Justin Rose. Sergio, at age thirty-seven, had failed four times to win major championships through a variety of calamities, and at times on Sunday, it appeared that this would be his fifth miss not to win when he was in contention. What is difficult for the golf fan to understand is the incredible pressure felt at the professional level in a major championship. The pressure is "x" times the pressure an amateur player would feel in competing for the club championship. Sergio was in a terrific match with Justin Rose at 6 under par as they marched on through the front nine. Both players had their ups and downs, but there wasn't much in it as they completed the 9th hole both at level par for their final round. It's quite common that the Master's actually begins on the back 9 of the final day, and everything preceding it is getting into a competitive position for that back-nine challenge.

The pressure cooker went off on the 10th tee, and the match became very complex. The 10th hole is a long par 4, where the object is to hit it as far as you can with a high shot that will roll down a series of hills to leave you with an iron shot between 160-175 yards uphill to a treacherous green. Rose stepped up to the tee and proceeded to "drop kick" a drive down the right side of the fairway. The drive is short (probably less than 200 yards) and is in the short rough, impossible to get the second shot on the green. Advantage Garcia! Garcia, who had been driving the ball with incredible power, stepped up to the tee and did almost exactly what Rose did—a pop-up drive to the right side of the fairway. It was a terrible shot, leaving him no chance of getting to the green. Advantage squandered! In Championship Golf, something like this is usually a very bad thing and certainly a bad omen with eight holes to play.

Sergio's next shot was even worse and ended up near the bushes on the right side of the fairway. He had taken an incredible amount of time over this shot and he clearly fanned on it, putting him a terrible position. In this position, only bad things can happen. In order to get to the green, Sergio had to navigate the bush and a tree; there was only a very small opening, as the ball had to be struck off a bare lie on top of the sand, with the tree inches away to his right. He hit a "miracle" shot onto the green—just getting the ball onto the green was an incredible achievement. The ball landed on the green and sailed about 25-feet, where it came to rest. Sergio then two-putted and made this improbable bogey and lost a shot to Rose, who was able to get up and down from a much easier position. Sergio could easily have lost the tournament on this hole, and a 7 or an 8 would have been possible if he had not executed as well as he did. One shot back and off to the 11th tee, Sergio hit another bad drive—this time way left of the fairway and pretty close to another clump of bushes. Memories of the past begin to creep in, not only to him but to the crowd as well, who had seen this happen before to Sergio.

He had no shot to the green but hit an amazing iron shot out of this clump of bushes to a position where he couldn't get up and down and make a miraculous par—now two back. As the two of them approached the infamous 12th hole over Rae's Creek, Sergio's mind must have been reduced to spaghetti—he had to pull it together. He hit a 9 iron a bit tentatively, and the shot just cleared the bunkers on the left side of the green—the shot could have gone into that bunker, so this was a bit of good luck. Sergio had now struggled for the last three holes, and it was beginning to look like another failure for him. My nerves would have been shot by now. On to the 13th tee, a birdie hole for most of the field. Sergio yanked his driver again, and this time there was no way to recover—the ball was in the creek on the left. He would take a drop and be hitting his third shot with no shot to the green (the tournament was slipping away). Once again, he hit another miraculous recovery shot, leaving him 40 yards to the front pin, where another miracle occurred—he made another brilliant pitch shot and holed the putt for an improbable par. Rose, who was in a much better position, could not convert his birdie attempt and also walked away with a par—a birdie from Rose would have given him a three-shot lead with five holes to play.

As the putt slid by, you could feel the emotion and momentum of the action; Sergio was dazed and hurting but still only two shots back. The momentum shifted to Sergio, and now was the time to take advantage of it. He pummeled his drive into the 15th fairway and then hit the shot of the tournament. The adrenalin had kicked in, and Sergio only had an 8 iron to the green. The 8 iron was struck straight and true right at the pin as it nearly hit the flagstick and bounded about 8 feet away. The putt was essential to cash in on the opportunity—it rolled in straight and true for an eagle 3 and when Rose could do no better than par, they were now tied. Rose and Sergio hit terrific tee shots on the 16th and both had great birdie opportunities. Rose converted and Sergio did not, leaving Rose with a one-shot lead going into 17. Rose could not close the deal. His tee shot on 17 sailed away; he could not manage to recover and recorded a painful bogey. Sergio shook off the missed opportunity on the 16th and slammed a driver down the middle of the fairway, making a relatively easy par to square the match again.

On the 18th green, Rose had a very makeable putt for birdie, and it just slid by on the left side–Rose stared at the putt in disbelief that it hadn't gone in. Sergio now had a putt to win the Master's of six feet behind the hole—you could almost cut the tension with a knife. Sergio missed the putt as well, and they went to the 18th for the first playoff hole. The playoff was over quickly—Rose hit another drive similar to the one he hit on No. 10 and the ball went sailing to the right into the dreaded pine straw. His approach to the green was completely blocked, and he could only make bogey from that position. Sergio hit a fabulous drive up the fairway. He only had a 7 iron to the green—momentum had completely shifted to him—he had two putts to win the Master's from 12 feet. He now felt that the demons that had prevented a major championship from his grasp were now gone. He holed the putt for birdie to finally break through to win the Master's.

Sergio's victory was a significant achievement because he overcame tremendous adversity in his own game from the 10th hole to the 13th hole and managed to stay in the match with some brilliant, creative shot-making. His birdie in the playoff was a statement that he won this tournament and he won it the hard way. While Rose had his opportunities, he didn't lose this tournament; it was snatched from him by a player who dug deep into his bag, overcame significant obstacles, and finally calmed a balky putter for a well-deserved victory. It was a fitting end to another great Master's event and hailed throughout the world of golf.

THE 2017 US OPEN

The 2017 US Open was held for the first time at Erin Hills. Erin Hills was a new venue for the USGA in the state of Wisconsin, where golfers are truly passionate about the game. Erin Hills would present an interesting challenge for the professionals without the controversy of the debacle at

Chambers Bay a few years earlier.

At the end of three rounds, five players had cumulative scores of more than 10 under par. Justin Thomas posted a 63, and he wasn't even the leader. This was a US Open where Dustin Johnson, Rory McElroy, Jason Day, Justin Rose, and Henrik Stenson all missed the cut. The US Open seemed to be just another tour stop, as the wide fairways and treeless plains of Erin Hills might have been a better host for the National Long Driving Contest. Rory McElroy had quipped early in the week that no one should complain about the heathery rough, as the fairways were wide enough. "If you can't hit those fairways, you wouldn't be playing on the weekend." How prophetic he was; he continuously missed the fairways as he missed the cut after a horrific opening round of 79. There are plenty of golf fans that will disagree with this assessment, but I believe that the US Open should be the most difficult test in the sport. When touring professionals are hitting pitching wedges for their second shot on a 500-yard par 4, something is really amiss. At the end of three rounds, there are usually only a few players under par with 18 holes to play. In this Open, 43 players were under par going into the last day. It seemed that the course was set up as the modern professional hits the ball so far that the 7700 yard + venue seemed to offer little challenge to these guys. Equipment and the modern golf ball are continuing to challenge the USGA to present a tough challenge and now iconic courses such as Merion may no longer qualify for US Open play. The final round would be very interesting as 14 players were within 6 shots of the lead.

It has been very difficult to watch the US Open on television these past few years, as Fox continues to deteriorate its presentation of the event. Fox doesn't know how to cover tee shots and fairway irons with its yardages—arrows all over your screen. Joe Buck may be an accomplished play-by-play guy, but he really needs to stick to football, as he will never be able to anchor this event in the broadcast booth. After a number of misfires, Fox hired many former professionals such as Curtis Strange and Paul Azinger to shore things up and provide some measure of credibility and experience. Their efforts are lost in translation with the supporting cast, many of whom have little or no experience. There is no Dan Hicks, Johnny Miller, Roger Maltbie, or Judy Rankin, all of whom brought considerable experience and empathy to the proceedings. My fear was that unless the final round produced an exciting conclusion, TV ratings would be down, and that this event was losing its luster as the premier event in major championships.

The final round produced an exciting conclusion, and Erin Hills was finally exonerated. The wind, which was virtually nonexistent in the preceding rounds, finally came up and blew hard and once again; par in the US Open became the standard. Justin Thomas, who was blasting his drives over 320 yards, was a little shorter on Sunday, and his power game became somewhat muted. Perhaps it was the curse of shooting 63 on Saturday, which set a new record of nine under par in US Open. All the contenders made valiant efforts, with excellent rounds from Hideki Matsuyama and Brian Harman. Harman grinded through his round and shot a respectable 72. He hung in there and played smartly throughout the day. Charlie Hoffman's short game left him on a few holes as he chunked a few chips to finish 8th with a 71 in the final round. Charley is eventually going to break through in one of these majors with this one and his fine showing in the Master's. Rickie Fowler just couldn't do anything special on Sunday, and I'm sure he was disappointed in a 7th-place finish, but he played very well. Patrick Reed also knocked on the door as he tried hard to storm out of the pack, but his game wasn't quite there to win his first major championship.

Brooks Koepka emerged as the victor, with a solid round characterized by making the tough putts under tremendous pressure and executing flawlessly down the stretch.

The final round produced the excitement that we had all expected, and Erin Hills demonstrated that it could host another Open. It would have been tougher if the wind had blown during the week, as it normally does. The setup was fair with wide fairways, penal rough, and the usual tricky pin placements. Then it will be on to Shinnecock Hills in Long Island, New York for 2018, where the world would be watching. The last Open held there in 2004 damaged this venue's reputation, as the greens burned out during the final round and there was some talk that another Open would not be played there. Fortunately, this would not be the case.

THE OPEN CHAMPIONSHIP

The 146th Open Championship was held at Royal Birkdale. Royal Birkdale is on of the gems on the Open circuit and one of three Open Championship venues in North West England located in Southport, north of Liverpool. The other two venues are Royal Lytham and St. Annes, and Royal Liverpool.

Chapter 15
ROYAL BIRKDALE HISTORY

Birkdale Golf Club was founded on July 30, 1889 at 23 Weld Road, Birkdale. The subscription price to join the club was $1.50 and the green fee was $.50. The first course was nine holes and was constructed for about $7. I doubt there was much construction, and the cost was probably placing flagsticks around the holes. The club was officially opened on October 5, 1889. Women were able to play three days a week and have always played a prominent role in the club.

In 1908, 18 holes were measured, and drainage was completed one year later. Golfers would no longer have to play in their wellies (rubber boots). In 1922, the club tried to buy the links but could not come up with $21,000. The land was sold to the Southport Corporation, and the owners offered a 99-year lease to the golf club. The clubhouse was completed in 1935.

The Open Championship was scheduled to be played there in 1940, but there was a global conflict going on called World War II and the area was being constantly bombed by the Germans. The first Open Championship at Birkdale was deferred until 1954. The King of England bestowed the title "Royal" on the club, and it became The Royal Birkdale Golf Club in 1951. It is interesting that an Englishman has never won an Open Championship at Royal Birkdale. The winners are:

1951: Peter Thompson (Australia), 1961: Arnold Palmer (United States), 1971: Lee Trevino (United States), 1976: Johnny Miller (United States), 1983: Tom Watson (United States), 1991: Ian Baker Finch (Australia), and 1998: Mark O'Meara (United States).

Chapter 16
FAMOUS SHOTS/ EVENTS

In the 1961 event, Arnold Palmer drove the ball under a small bush on the 15th (currently the 16th hole). At this critical time in the final round of the championship, Palmer chose to go for the green from under the bush, which seemed like an impossible shot. The line of the ball was virtually unplayable. Palmer slashed a 6 iron from under the bush onto the green to preserve his lead. The shot was so implausible that a plaque to commemorate the shot marks it.

In 1969 the Ryder Cup match between the United States and Great Britain and Ireland ended in a tie when Jack Nicklaus conceded a putt to Tony Jacklin to halve their match. The competition ended in 12-12 tie, which has been memorialized as "the Concession." The United States team held on to the Cup with the tie, but the gesture was a remarkable act of sportsmanship.

Although my experience at Birkdale is not famous or even important, it was a shot I cannot forget. I approached the 4th hole, which is a par 3 of 206 yards with a 2 iron in my hands. I don't think I've hit more than fifty 2 irons in my entire life, and this particular Titleist 2 iron is still in my bag that resides in Brian's wine cellar, with my set of Titleist blades. It was the best 2 iron I ever hit in my life, and the group on the tee was convinced that the ball was "in" the hole and were very excited. It was hard to see much from the tee, since there was a still a bit of haze and fog, but the ball certainly looked like it was right at the hole. I was reserving my excitement for the reality, as about ¼ of the ball lay over the hole. The wind was blowing against us, so I knew it was never going in. After waiting the required 10 seconds, I settled for the birdie. Getting a hole in hole at Birkdale would have been the highlight of my golfing career, but it was not to be. My birdie on number 4 is not famous or even important, but it was an unforgettable shot for me.

The players in the 146th Open Championship either left their drivers home or covered them up for the opening round. This is a golf course that has eliminated the "power game" completely. The course is a par 70 and measured out at 7,156 (short by today's standards) so why no drivers? The answer is simple—the placement of the fairway bunkers requires that these bunkers must be avoided at all costs. There are only a few holes where these bunkers can easily be carried, and the par 5, 17th hole is actually a driver hole. It is also the easiest hole on the course.

Round 1 started with some pretty awful weather, with some balls hit out of bounds on the difficult par 4 opening hole of 448 yards. The weather turned for the better by mid-morning, and the scoring started to drop precipitously. By day's end, 40 players were even par or better, and 61 were +1 or better. The +1's included Rory McElroy and Dustin Johnson. McElroy started the round looking bored, with his head somewhere else, and at one point in the round was +5, but after a few good drives and iron shots, his spirits seemed to turn positive, and all of a sudden, he was the focused champion that he has been in the past. With the driver out of his hand, Dustin Johnson's major weapon was nonexistent, and he plodded through the round mostly at +3, but a late flurry, including a birdie on 17, got him back into contention. On the par 5, 17th, his drive was 335 yards, leaving him only 189 yards for his second shot. (Mind-boggling!)

Jordan Speith was a logical choice to contend for this championship. He is "sneaky" long and thinks his way around the golf course, especially one that presents the setup that Birkdale offered. Brooks Koepka was the co-leader with Speith at the end of day 1 and brimming with confidence fresh off his US Open victory. He holed a bunker shot on the 17th to join Speith as the leader at 5 under par. The shot of the day belonged to Charlie Hoffman, who holed out from the bushes on the first hole. The shot was highly improbable, and it not only found the green, but it went in for an eagle 2. Hoffman continues to knock on the door in major championships. Speith continued to lead the tournament through the first three rounds, but Sunday would prove to be the ultimate challenge.

We thought that the 2016 Open Championship was the best in history with Henrik Stenson and Phil Mickelsen in an 18-hole competition that lapped the field at Royal Troon. Stenson came out on top in that event in a thrilling finish. It was perceived by golf fans that the 2016 event could not be surpassed in drama and competitiveness. Well, it just so happened that the 2017 event at Birkdale might have one-upped the 2016 event. Jordan Speith held the lead or was tied for the lead for first 66 holes of the tournament. He and Matt Kuchar were locked in combat at 8 under par as they approached the tough 13th hole. What happened next was pretty unbelievable. Speith hit his tee shot at least 100 yards off line in deep rough, which is the one place on this hole you just cannot be. After spending some time looking for the ball, the position was declared an unplayable lie, and negotiations began as to where the drop could take place. The decision on the drop seemed to take forever and had to be mentally distracting to Kuchar, who was properly positioned in the fairway. After almost 25 minutes, Speith hit his 3rd shot from the driving range, and he didn't like the strike—it looked like it wasn't going to carry the rough on the right side. Miraculously, the shot barely carried the very bad stuff, but he faced a very difficult chip shot (his 4th shot); the shot had to be close to give him the opportunity to make bogey and only lose a shot to par. He hit a terrific shot, bounding over a mound and stopping it about 8 feet from the hole. He had to make this putt to avoid a two-shot deficit with five holes to play, as Kuchar made par.

I'm sure that Speith went into the memory bank, and visions of the collapse at Augusta entered his mind. Was this the place he was going to lose the Open Championship? At this point in golf and in most competitive events, the game speeds up rapidly, often diminishing the player's skills to the level of rank amateur, and bad things can happen and often do happen. I don't know what went through Speith's psyche, but I believe he put on the brakes and tossed away the memory of the 12th hole at Augusta while he contemplated that chip shot on 13. He went back and forth with his caddie, Michael Greller, to wipe off the club and slow things down. That chip shot and the putt that followed were the keys to winning the championship, although the putt was for a bogey 5, and he was going to be behind anyway. It certainly could have been a lot worse; he could have made a very big number from his position on the driving range. He holed the putt, regrouped, and trudged on to the 14th hole. He was now one shot behind in a tournament he had led from the start to this point. Many players would have collapsed in a heap of negativity. Instead of being downcast, his tremendous bogey on the 13th seemed to provide a significant mental boost, leading to a barrage of shots that would follow. His tee shot on the par-3 14th hole almost went in, and he had an easy birdie putt to get back into a tie for the lead as Kuchar made another par. He then proceeded to eagle the 15th hole with a spectacular putt from 30 feet. Kuchar seemed to know that this train was coming, and there was nothing he could do about it. Kuchar played very well and within himself, trying as best he could to keep up with Speith's uncanny shot-making and putting as they headed for the house. Speith just poured it on with his putter, and all he had to do was to avoid another tee shot like the 13th.

On the 18th hole, a 470-yard par 4, he laced an iron 250 yards right down the middle and followed it with another iron onto to the green, carrying 220 yards. Two putts down and it was over for Speith's 3rd major championship victory, placing him in elite company with Jack Nicklaus with three majors at age twenty-four, and one more than Tiger Woods. I don't think anyone has ever seen a player roar back to go 5 under par over the last 6 holes in a major championship. Speith's caddie, Michael Greller, deserves a lot of credit for sticking with his man and keeping his spirits up in some pretty tough moments on the 13th hole. The focus required to maintain concentration and the "eye on the prize" was quite remarkable. I haven't seen this type of mental toughness since Tiger Woods, who seemed to be able to "will" himself to victory with an assortment of creative shots. A series of tweets from Jack Nicklaus, Tiger Woods, and Zach Johnson reiterated the idea that Speith's determination and execution created an extraordinary event.

It was quite a special Open Championship with a lot of good feelings all around as the field played very well on a course that was meticulously prepared and more than worthy of this major championship. Matt Kuchar never backed down and did not lose this event—Speith would not be denied.

THE PGA CHAMPIONSHIP

The 2017 PGA Championship was held at Quail Hollow Country Club in Charlotte, North Carolina. The last major championship of 2017 would be determined in the "hotbed" of golf in the Carolinas, where there are so many wonderful venues to play. The famous Pinehurst with eight championship courses, including Pinehurst No. 2, is about an hour's drive down the road. Pinehurst No. 2 has been a US Open championship site and the venue where Payne Stewart won in 1998.

PGA Championships in recent years have been held at courses that have undergone significant design changes to attempt to challenge the modern professional game. 2017 would be no exception, as renovations and the club supervised by the PGA of America implemented alterations to the course.

Quail Hollow has been the host of the Wells Fargo Championship, a PGA tour event, which was formerly known as the Wachovia Open. It's appropriate to have a major championship in the southeast part of the country, where golf remains very popular vacation spot throughout the Carolinas. The Quail Club decided to make a concerted effort for this event, through a redesign of some of the holes, replacing the greens with a new surface, and redoing the bunkers. It was a pretty risky proposition, given that the task had to be done in less than a year. The entire reconstruction was actually accomplished in 89 days, and it would be interesting to see how the greens would hold up in hot, humid conditions. The surface of the greens was replaced with a Bermuda hybrid grass that is genetically engineered, and the initial reviews were very positive. The 1st, 2nd and 5th holes were redesigned for length and would be tougher than the experience at the Wells Fargo event. The 1st hole is a good opening par 4 of 500 yards. Quail will also be the host of the 2021 President's Cup, and it seems that the course layout will probably change to ensure that the Green Mile holes are factors in determining the outcome of match play games.

I recall playing Whistling Straits in Kohler, Wisconsin a year before the 2015 PGA Championship was held there, and I thought that the professionals would have a lot of difficulty there. I thought even par or a few under par would be the winning score. I couldn't have been more wrong in my analysis, as the professionals with the 7500-yard layout with its myriad number of bunkers and challenging conditions actually produced very good scoring. This event was also the site of Dustin Johnson's exploits with the infamous "bunker or no bunker" shot on the 18th hole and 72nd hole of the championship, which cost him the championship.

Quail Hollow is set up to present an interesting test, and I thought the professionals would "go low" in this event. I thought that 19 or 20 under par might be the winning score. The course favored the "gorilla" drivers of the professional tour with a number of 300-yard drives and renders the course defenseless. The focus of the course featured the last three closing holes, termed "The Green Mile." The "Mile" starts with the 506-yard par 4, with a very narrow fairway for a hole of this length, requiring two accurate shots to the green. The 17th hole is a par 3 of 228 yards, with water in a menacing position on the left side of the green. It may force the player to draw the ball from right to left, but any shot missed on the right will make chipping interesting, depending on the pin positions. The finishing 18th hole is a beautifully designed hole of 495 yards, as a par 4 with a creek meandering along the left side of the fairway. The creek will be in play, so driving position off the tee is important. Nerves would be tested by these holes as the leaders complete their final rounds. Weather conditions would be important as well. Hot and humid conditions would potentially add more length to the tee shots. Potential thunderstorms would bring rain and take the sting out of the fast greens and enable the players to be more aggressive to attack the pins. Early favorites were Rory McElroy, who had previously won here on tour. Hideki Matsuyama was getting close, as he continued to play well in major championships with his significant length off the tee. Other notables that could be factors in the event were Dustin Johnson, Bubba Watson, Brooks Koepka, and Justin Thomas. Jordan Speith had to be considered as a factor, coming off his spectacular win at the Open Championship.

The tournament provided a pretty exciting finish with the Green Mile (16th through 18th holes). Justin Thomas came out of the pack to best a number of contenders by two shots. Kevin Kinser had led through three rounds at six under, but a few wayward shots in the final round cost him dearly and ended up in seventh place, four shots back. His final-round playing partner, Chris Stroud, finished ninth. Thomas posted his eight-under score and watched intently as the contenders were unable to close the gap, coming in as the Green Mile did most of them in. Golf can be a crazy game and the omen for Justin's victory was a putt on the 10th hole for par that took exactly ten seconds to drop into the cup. Thomas had looked away, thinking the putt was going to hang on the lip of the cup, and turned back as the seconds ticked away and then…plop—it went in. Thomas played flawlessly and took full advantage of his length off the tee to make the necessary birdies and didn't flinch coming down the stretch. The fairway bunker on the 16th hole proved to be a welcome spot for a number of the contenders needing birdies to catch Thomas, and no one could get over the hump. I really appreciated Thomas' approach shot to the 18th green out of a patch of spinach from 88 yards out to get it on the green and seal the victory. He made a difficult shot look very routine as he nonchalantly smacked a lob wedge (or something equivalent) on the green. It was clear that the adrenaline was there, and he had no doubt that he could execute that shot.

My predictions for this event were off the mark. I thought the professionals would go very low due to their ability to drive the ball a long way. I also thought that the southeast would have a thunderstorm or two that would dump some rain on the course and slow the greens down. The PGA and the Quail Hollow club have to be pleased that the course setup presented a significant challenge to the players. I had predicted that the long-hitting "gorillas" on the tour would win the event, and Justin Thomas is one of those players. My favorite for the event was McElroy, with competition from Dustin Johnson, Hideki Matsuyama, and Henrik Stensen. A number of long hitters were factors, as Patrick Reed and Rickie Fowler had chances at the end of the tournament, but they could not conquer the Green Mile. Matsuyama had an up and down round and couldn't catch Thomas. He made a number of great shots to stay in the competition. It was a tough day for 3rd-round round leaders Kevin Kinser and Chris Stroud. Kinser's chance was lost early in the final round as he hit his approach shot into the creek, recording a double bogey there. Kinser had hit a similar shot to that hole but was saved from the creek by the 3-inch cut of rough. The 3 iron in the final round had no chance and faded directly into the creek. He ended his round on 18, needing an eagle 2, but his low-to-no- probability approach shot of 203 yards found a watery grave in the creek, which runs all the way to the hole.

The pre-tournament hype from the PGA of America and the club predicted that the toughness of the Green Mile would be a major factor in the event. It's highly unusual that these predictions are ever correct, but this time they were. The Green Mile claimed a number of victims, including Jason Day, who made an 8 on the hole on Saturday as he plunked his drive into "nowhereville" and simply could not recover.

The par-3 17th hole at 199 yards was tough as well, yielding few birdies, with the water on the left actually preventing the players from pin-seeking. The right side of the hole offered no respite, especially as any shot missed to the right ended in collection areas reminiscent of the evils of Pinehurst No. 2 (just an hour down the road). The 16th hole was no bargain either, with the fairway bunkers placed perfectly to catch the tee shots of the "gorillas."

What I find interesting from this event is that a new coalition of players is emerging who are all in their mid-twenties: Speith, Thomas, Dustin Johnson, etc. Patrick Reed, Rickie Fowler, and others cheer for each other's success. Speith, who finished the tournament at 3 over par, was greenside at the end to congratulate Thomas on his victory. There seems to be a "changing of the guard," where experienced winners such as Phil Mickelsen, Jim Furyk, Matt Kuchar, Ernie Els and others will probably be eclipsed by this new group as the professional game continues to convert to the need for length off the tee. These youngsters have nerves of steel and are fearless in their approach. These championship venues are now over 7500 yards and seem to be changing the nature of competition. This new group may also end the dominance of the European in the Ryder Cup with their respect for each other and stellar play.

LESSONS-2017 AND BEYOND

One of the things that amazes me about golf is that I'm been playing the game for over forty years, and I'm still learning how to play the game. This really drives me a little nuts. I played competitive basketball from grammar school and high school to the collegiate level and didn't stop playing until about five years ago. If I didn't pick up a basketball for weeks on end, I could still go out today and drain 3-pointers from anywhere without any practice. If I did that with my golf game, I suspect I would lose 10-15 strokes on my handicap.

I decided to take lessons two years ago to try and stem the degradation of my driving distance. It was getting difficult to compete when you were 40-50 yards behind your competitor's tee shot. I had been playing golf a certain way for a very long period of time, and my swing was anything but conventional. I couldn't emulate a professional, and I'm sure no one could emulate me. I was determined to change this situation and take lessons on a consistent basis until I achieved a few objectives, such as driving distance. I spent the first year with my coach improving my posture over the golf ball, changing grip pressure; we did alignment drills and even fooled with the putting. I had always been a good putter, but my teacher didn't really like my technique, and so changes had to be made. My attitude was positive—

I was going to seek the greater good of playing the game with the proper technique. My only request to my teacher was that we introduce these changes gradually so that I could maintain or attempt to maintain my current handicap of 5. The problem with this attitude is that it is a bit of a double-edged sword. Changing things gradually is more difficult, since the changes have to be "trusted" to execute the new techniques. If you don't trust the new changes, you will revert to the way you've been playing, and the changes will take a lot longer to implement, if they ever are. Another philosophy about changes in the golf swing is that I believe you have to have a foundation to start with that is stable, reliable, and maintainable. You simply cannot throw away the foundation and start to make changes without understanding the potential outcomes. You also have to tune out the "peer pressure" aspects of looking for equipment solutions, instructional guides and magazines, and hardware gadgets that promise to be the magic elixir of a new golf swing. You can look at Jordan Speith's swing in a sequenced portfolio in Golf Digest, but there is absolutely no chance that you can learn anything from looking at those photographs. There is a literally an infinite amount of printed material, videos, and TV shows promising to enable your golf swing, but I can guarantee you that you will never make any progress permanently by referring to these sources. You have to hope that you have some athletic ability that will translate into serendipity with a golf swing. Baseball, tennis, and hockey players are blessed with tremendous eye/hand coordination, so golf is an easier challenge for them. Football players not so much, but quarterbacks are very good golfers due to their need for coordination in throwing the ball to their receivers.

John Brodie, former quarterback of the San Francisco 49'ers, made it to the Senior Professional Tour after he retired from football and was very competitive on that tour, winning one event. Many NFL quarterbacks are consistent winners or place very well in amateur events.

At the end of my first year of lessons, I was playing consistently well in the normal $5 Nassau weekend games, but my performance in competition remained inconsistent. I would have a great practice round and break 80, and then shoot myself out of the tournament with a 91 on the first day. In competition, you cannot "miss" a shot that will result in a double bogey or worse; scoring matters and unforced errors are the bane of a good ball-striking round. Nevertheless, I felt I had made enough progress to continue on the quest and meet my objectives. My objectives were to maintain a 6 handicap or less and to be no more that 5 shots off that handicap in tournament play. We had spent almost the entire year working on my posture and increasing the arc in my backswing for greater distance and control. These things for the most part were accomplished, except for the driver. The driver has been the worst club in my bag since I started playing golf over 40 years ago. I have no slice or a hook and most of my playing partners call me "boring" since I'm in the fairway most of the time. The problem is the lack of club head speed caused the lack of a shoulder turn to increase the size of the swing path to produce the desired increase in yardage. The big change in my putting technique was that I was no longer hunched over the ball and my posture was no erect in striking the putts allowing for more control over the line of the putt. It was about a year ago that my coach found a better position in Oregon, so I would soon be without a teacher.

His replacement was introduced to me and I decided to give him a "test-drive" to see if he might be able to take me to the next level. We had an interview where I inventoried my skills and my issues with the notion that we would give him a shot. The first lesson on the range was a true revelation. It was as if I was started all over again, but I quickly game to the conclusion that this had to be the next step in a long avenue to progress. The big change was pretty fundamental, but I had been swinging incorrectly for years. My swing path was either out to in or straight back, which would naturally restrict distance. We were now going to focus on swinging in to out, which would generate more club head speed and hopefully more distance. The in to out swing was a simple swing change for iron shots, and almost immediately, iron shots were going further. Distances had to be adjusted by a full club for most shots. I was dumbfounded by this change. I had been watching the PGA Tour, and every professional swings in to out, without exception. I couldn't believe that I had watched these guys for years and didn't pick up on this simple technique. The professionals and very good low-handicap players produce significant club head speed with the out to in swing, which enables them to turn their bodies towards their target. The modern ball and modern equipment enables them to drive the golf ball over 300 yards with regularity. It seems a bit ridiculous to see professionals hitting 5 irons 200 yards and fairway woods 275 yards or more but that it the state of the modern game.

Although I was a good putter, I had relied on the same

poor technique and actually putted the ball out to in, just as I hit the rest of my clubs. I often wondered why I missed so many putts on the left side without pulling the putter. We placed two tees on the ground where the putter would release to get rid of the out to in putt. If the stroke touched or hit the tees, you knew automatically that the putter was still out to in. This drill would enable me to hit these putts from the inside and have a much better chance of holing more putts, especially inside of 10 feet.

The concept of in to out is so basic that it really annoys me that it has taken 40 years to have this figured out for me. Understanding the concept is one thing, but executing it time after time doesn't come easily for me. The next key phrase in this basic tenet is "Trust It." Trusting the change is more difficult that it seems. When you've had success hitting the golf ball incorrectly for years, it is a tough task to risk hitting the ball correctly with poor results. The difference is trusting the ability to execute and not reverting to the old bad habits, irrespective of how successful they were in the past. It is now the beginning of a long journey, which can be traveled only with a lot of practice, patience, and persistence.

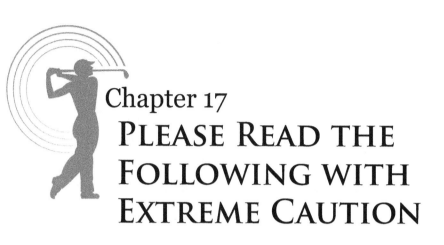

Chapter 17
PLEASE READ THE
FOLLOWING WITH
EXTREME CAUTION

THE SHANKS—PART II

The dark side of the golf game is the world of the shank. We covered the shank in my first book and it needs to be repeated so that we are forever vigilant on our golf swings. To recap: The shank in golf is "striking the golf ball with the base of the shaft of the club just above the club head, causing the ball to go off sharply to the right."

The shank is equivalent to the unspeakable four-letter word that we dare not utter in front of our parents or children. You would not wish the shank on your worst enemy in the world. It is a vile term that evokes fear and trepidation in the psyche of every golfer who has played the game, including the professional. It is equivalent to a bad case of chicken pox or measles and if not eradicated causes anxiety, depression, embarrassment, hopelessness, and incredible misery to a golfer. When we think of how many times a day we hear the constant barrage of four-letter words, the word "shank" is never uttered on the golf course. The inability to cure the shank on the golf course is grounds for termination from further participation. It not only affects the player with the shanks but impacts fellow participants. It impacts the psyche, routine, and technique of any participant that observes the shank.

While there are cures for the shanks, there are no symptoms. The shank merely appears and grips the player in total fear, taking hold of its victim and shaking the player to the foundation of everything ever learned about the game. The shanks remove the entire foundation of a player's cumulative knowledge about the golf swing. It is equivalent to a crash of your computer that erases all of its stored data.

The immediate fix for the shank is to execute the following formula:

1. Do not accept the shank as something that is going to repeat itself. Treat the shanked shot as an aberration to the game that is never going to happen again.

2. Do not give in to the notion that there is something horribly wrong with your golf swing. It might be true, but you cannot accept this notion as truth.

3. Take a deep breath and exhale.

4. Deny that the shank ever happened.

5. The shot following the shank can never be another shank. Close the club face and take another deep breath.

6. Be prepared to sacrifice another shot with a shot that will hook the ball left with the closed club face.

7. Executing this routine will eliminate the possibility of shanking another shot.

8. Pray that items 1-7 will work.

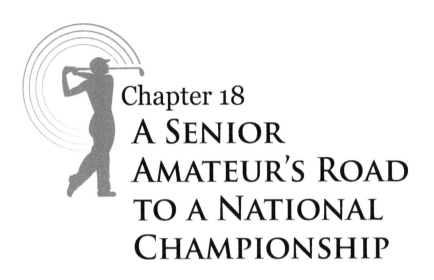

Chapter 18
A SENIOR AMATEUR'S ROAD TO A NATIONAL CHAMPIONSHIP

Doug Benton had just turned 58 years old. He was contemplating his future and next steps in life. He had reached his peak earnings in his role as Chief Executive Officer of the Second National Bank of Silicon Valley. It was time for him to retire, and he wanted to leave the bank with his legacy intact. He decided that he wanted to leave the bank completely and had no desire to do the fashionable routine of stepping up to the Chairman of the Board of Directors. The bank had flourished after ten years under his leadership; he had groomed his successor carefully, and an orderly transition was underway to pass the baton. His business career had been a successful one and he didn't want any potential future events to tarnish his achievements. He would maintain his external positions in the two public company boards to stay in touch with the business world. His personal financial security was assured, and he had conservatively managed his finances carefully and provided the security for his family that would provide the freedom of plotting the next steps in his life. His three children had all graduated from university and were self-sufficient and in the process of launching their own careers in Southern California, Texas, and Arizona. His wife, Becky, was the stay-at-home mom and provided the necessary guidance and support for the children while he labored long and hard to build the bank and position it for success. The years flew by as he globetrotted to build the bank's position, as the Silicon Valley economy grew significantly throughout the last 25 years.

He was satisfied with his business career, and it was time to focus on a new chapter in his life. He had spent the better part of the last year planning the next chapter. Most people are ill prepared for retirement. Doug had a frenetic schedule throughout the last 30 years and now the future was a bit unsettling. He was sure that he wanted a respite from the vigor of the corporate world, but the future was uncertain. He knew he needed a challenge—something that would bring fulfillment and focus to his life. He also knew that Becky would be supportive in whatever endeavor he decided to pursue. As Doug and Becky passed through the accolades and going-away parties, he started to home in on a new path and different direction. His decision would be to pursue a new career in the world of competitive amateur golf.

Doug was a good player with a 4 handicap. He had been playing throughout his life at recreational golf at his local club—The Arcadian Club in South San Francisco. He had played a lot of golf throughout his life, starting as a junior golfer where he grew up in South Carolina. He had played some golf in college but was not good enough to make the varsity team as a starter. He played in many club competitions, and a number of PGA Pro-Am events. He had ability, but his business career always came first, and serious competition was never a part of his game. Why competitive golf?

Doug felt that his game had the necessary foundation and had played long enough to understand the challenge that potentially lay ahead. Competitive golf has a pyramid of playing the game for fun to the top of the game as played on the professional tour circuit. Most golfers simply play the game for fun and camaraderie. The Rules of Golf in this regard are usually applied liberally or potentially even ignored. "Fun" golf then turns a bit more serious as games are played for nominal amounts of money in various formats, and then the rules become serious matters. The next level of play is for golfers who want to play for a lot of money because they have the discretionary resources to do so. High rollers and gamblers enter this fray, but it's still the same amateur play—only by players with a lot of discretionary money to wager. The next level of play is what Doug wanted to play. He wanted to compete consistently and in tournament conditions with players of his own skill level. Mixing fun play with tournament play would be a distraction to the challenge of competition, so Doug had to consider his approach to this decision. He had to affirm that he was taking the right approach to consider whether he could transition his game to a completely competitive level. The accolades of a business career would soon be a distant past as Doug and Becky swept through a number of retirement parties. Best wishes and questions about his next chapter were evident throughout the events put on in his honor. When asked about what he was going to do in retirement, he responded with noncommittal statements about taking some time off to think and reflect. In fact, he was grinding internally about his approach to his decision to play competitive golf as an amateur.

Three weeks after a family visit to South Carolina to see his parents, Doug decided to start on the quest. He decided the first thing he had to do was to play a lot of golf and see exactly where his game stood. He started to play every day and sometimes twice a day. One of the good things about playing frequently is that your game develops a rhythm, tempo and consistency. All aspects of the game are tested, and feedback is immediate. It was September, and Arcadia was in immaculate condition with running fairways, fast greens, and consistent bunker sand. The fog that shrouds San Francisco most of the summer gives way to consistent sunshine during the fall that optimizes playing conditions. Doug would play 25 rounds in the month of September, which is more golf than most of the population plays in an entire year. The initial rounds showed some variability with rounds in the 70s, 80s, and a few poor low 90s. By the end of September, the last 8 rounds were all in the low 70s and his handicap was reduced from 4 to 1.5. Golf handicaps are computed by averaging the best 10 rounds out of the last 20 rounds played. It is almost inconceivable that a low-handicapper can reduce a handicap from 4 to 1.5 in one month! It was unheard of. It's equivalent to a 25-handicapper reducing his handicap to 12—handicap reduction is a geometric progression. Most low-handicappers with a 4 handicap would spend an entire year just getting their handicap to 3, let alone 1.5. Doug was not only encouraged, he was stoked—handicaps play no part in competitive golf on the Senior Amateur tour, just as on the professional tours. The handicap functions as a requirement to qualify to enter a Senior Amateur. There are many tournaments and functions that track score on a "net" basis, including handicap, but these events are designed to encourage participation at all levels of competition. Doug was not interested in competing at those tournaments and wanted to compete at the highest amateur level, which is gross score only. Doug had passed the first test on his quest. He had reduced his handicap significantly, and the next test would be to reaffirm his commitment. The commitment required an acknowledgement that he would have to improve his game to a level of consistency that would hold up in tournament conditions. This would require a significant commitment to practice and the time to do it. Doug reaffirmed his commitment to take the next step, which would be a mental challenge but necessary to fulfill his ambitions.

Doug knew that in order to achieve consistency with his driver, he would have to fix the big loop in his back swing. The driver was the best club in his bag, but the loop in his swing introduced potential significant variability with shots that could veer both right and left. He was a pretty long hitter and could produce drives in the 260-300-yard range. Doug really pulled the club well back to beyond the parallel position in the backswing. It's really difficult to figure out how to improve when you've been playing well for a long period of time. Swings are developed early, and adjustments and experiments can produce disastrous results. His iron play was similarly impacted by the loop, as he has great length with his irons, but the same fault would have to be addressed to produce the required consistency. Doug was just a so-so putter. He could make 5- and 6-footers with remarkable prowess, but long-putting was another matter. His putting beyond 15 feet was not good enough to excel at the next level of competitive golf. PGA professionals average about 28 putts per round, and Doug was over 30 per round.

Doug spent a considerable amount of time and practice and came to the conclusion that he would have to engage a professional teacher to address these weaknesses. The weaknesses that he assessed in his game would be enviable for most players, but those players were not on the Senior Amateur tour. The next major decision was to decide how to engage a professional teacher. The key to selecting a teacher required setting criteria as to how make this selection. Doug had to find a teaching professional that he could trust to address his weaknesses without tearing his game apart. He had the skills and foundation of the golf swing, and now he had to find someone who could capitalize on those skills and fine-tune them for the competitive game on the Senior Amateur Tour. In *Golf in the Kingdom* by Michael Murphy, Murphy meets the ethereal Shivas Irons, whose swing was perfect and reduced the swing to a series of mental exercises. Doug had read the book, but the Shivas Irons approach wasn't going to work for him. He needed someone who could assess his swing foundation and make the appropriate adjustments. He needed an empathetic teacher who could harness his assets and fine-tune his game. Doug had no illusions. He knew that the effort would be time-consuming, and results would not be apparent for quite some time.

Doug needed to a select a teacher. This selection would be a difficult decision. He hadn't taken lessons since he was a collegiate player in South Carolina. He was satisfied with his game as it was, but he knew that the next level would require additional training to get the consistency needed to compete at the highest level of amateur golf. The teaching professional at Arcadian was Tom Smollett. Tom's reputation at the club was pretty good, but although he knew Doug, he wasn't very familiar with his game. Doug decided to have a conversation with Tom about his approach to instruction without revealing his plans. He wanted to get to know Tom better and see if a relationship could develop to the point where he felt he could help. Tom was well respected at the club and had been a PGA teaching professional for the past 20 years. They sat down in the club bar for a round of drinks, and Doug started to talk about his game and some things he felt he had to work on. Tom listened intently and seemed eager to help. They decided to meet on the range the next day where Tom could take a serious look at Doug's swing mechanics. Doug needed to assess the situation carefully and ensure that if he selected Tom, he would be empathetic to his level of capability and what areas could be improved.

The next day they met on the range as Doug was warming up, hitting some wedges and short irons. It was a crisp, wonderful September morning, and Doug was feeling fresh and limber but wondering how Tom would assess him. Tom showed up right on time and proceeded to observe Doug's routine and swing. He simply asked Doug to continue while he assessed warm-up. After proceeding through the longer irons and then the driver, Tom paused and asked Doug, "What are you feeling throughout the swing?" It was a rather odd question and Doug responded that he felt fine and was satisfied with his tempo. Tom immediately noticed the length of his backswing and could pick up some variability as Doug moved passed parallel at the top of the backswing. He didn't say anything about it and continued to observe without providing any input. Doug was an engaging individual and was clearly looking for some feedback, but none was forthcoming. After about 30 minutes of watching Doug hitting balls with all the clubs in the bag, Tom had a few ideas, but he wasn't ready to impart them.

They retired to the lounge for a sandwich, and still Tom

was not really forthcoming as to what he thought. He was obviously waiting for Doug to make some comments about the practice session and his swing. Doug stated that he thought he had a pretty good swing foundation but needed to make some adjustments to get the consistency he was looking for. Tom asked about the motivation behind the needed improvements. Tom told Doug that it was important that he needed to understand what Doug was trying to achieve with his game. If it were just a few adjustments to play better with his group and take some wagers home, that would be one thing. If he was going to do something different with his game, then significant adjustments might be required to get to the next level of competitive golf. Unlike other sports, adjustments are relatively easy to execute if you have a great foundation. The closest sport I can think of in making adjustments that are similar to golf is baseball. Although I've personally never been a serious baseball player, batters are continuously tinkering with their swings. It seems that baseball is more difficult, since the variable presented by the pitcher adds significant complexity to the dynamics of hitting. In golf, swing adjustments are difficult because a player has developed a routine of striking the ball in a certain way and has acquired significant muscle memory. Changing that muscle memory requires months and months of practice, and there are no guarantees that something totally different may influence the swing, causing further variability.

Doug had been playing for over 40 years, so he knew all these things. He had to come clean with Tom and disclose his goals and objectives for the potential assignment. He finally told Tom that he wanted to devote full time to playing on the California Senior Amateur Tour and eventually try to compete for a USGA national championship. Tom chuckled, and he was slightly surprised at the revelation but readily understood the task at hand. Tom was an accomplished player in his own right and had qualified for the USGA Mid-Amateur in 1980 at Hill Country Club in Rochester, New York. His thoughts flashed back for a minute to the elation of qualifying for the event, but he lost in his first match to a car salesman from Minnesota named Todd McGregor, who bested him 3 and 2 in the first round of match play.

Tom now needed to respond to Doug's comments and propose the next step. Tom looked up from his glass and addressed Doug. "It's not going to be easy, but you have the foundation and skills to pull it off. It's just going to take a lot of hard work. You will have to be patient and persistent. There will be setbacks and shocks but it's possible for you to achieve your objective." Doug wanted specifics as to what needed to change and how the changes could be effected. Tom stated, "I noticed a few things in your backswing—alignment, weight shifting, and some other things, but it's early days. If you want to continue, I'd like to spend some more time and continue the assessment."

Doug asked Tom about next steps. "If we agree to work together, I'll do a more detailed assessment, and we can discuss the approach of building the swing changes a step at a time to capitalize on your foundation. If the change produces the desired results, we'll move to the next area that requires improvement."

Doug asked how long this would take. Tom replied that he had no idea how long it would take, but that the only way forward would be to get started. Tom stated that Doug should join the Tour anyway and work on his game while he was competing. The knowledge gained from the competitions would add value to the work that they would do together. Doug liked this idea, and he was beginning to develop confidence and a rapport with Tom. He decided to seriously consider the proposal and get back to Tom in a few days. He went home to have a talk with Becky. He really needed her to agree to the amount of time and travel involved, since he would be traveling all over the state to compete. He had discussed the original decision with her, and now it was coming to fruition as a possibility, so he needed her support. Becky had just taken up golf on her own and was still in the novice stage, taking lessons and playing at Arcadia. They discussed the balance required to maintain their lives and priorities together. They agreed that family came first and if Doug could maintain that priority in their lives, she would be supportive.

Doug was excited about the opportunity and decided he was going to give it a shot and commit to Tom's approach. He felt his game was good enough to get started, and hopefully Tom would help him to achieve his ultimate goals. It was going to be another challenge, just like building the bank. He would inform Tom tomorrow that he was "in." Doug really had to define what "in" meant. What were his expectations? Would he take instruction from Tom and execute it? Would he try to execute changes and adjustments, even if they caused him to play poorly? Changes and adjustments to a golf swing usually result in what I would call "significant qualification time." Significant qualification time involves embracing the changes and adjustments recommended by the teaching professional and then put in the necessary practice time to develop the muscle memory to execute the change. This requirement is easy to understand logically, but the mind doesn't work that way. You have been playing golf for a very long period of time and developed a pretty good skill level. Why would you risk that to make changes, with no guarantee that the changes will be successful? The changes are meant to improve the swing and bring it to another level, but there is no guarantee. You have to have the confidence and commitment that the changes will be successful and take the positive approach. Golf can be a "sea of negativity" as the brain tells you that you're already very good and you don't need these changes. In fact, as you start playing competitively, you will revert to what got you to this place and actually ignore these changes or fail to execute them under competitive pressure.

All of these concepts raced through Doug's mind, and he tossed them around in his head. He had to decide, and he decided that no matter how hard it was going to be mentally, he was going to turn over his game to Tom. He knew that this was going to push him into different waters. As a seasoned and successful business executive, the concept of accountability was extremely important, and he never turned over significant business decisions to his subordinates. The buck stopped with him, as he was accountable for the business results of the bank to the board of directors and ultimately the shareholders of the company. He rationalized logically that although he was hiring Tom to be his golf teacher, he would take full responsibility and accountability for the results he would achieve. He would have to fight the mental battles of change and different techniques to improve his skill set. Tom had to be viewed as an expert consultant who could provide the necessary tools for Tom to achieve his objectives in golf. Many professional players (not all) fail at understanding these concepts. Despite their significant skill, the game of golf at the professional level is very difficult, and the difference is always mental. Many professionals are constantly changing teachers, looking for a panacea to move up the leader boards. They are playing golf for a living and really are no different from a chief executive of a company. In this case, they are playing to make a living and provide for their families. Tiger Woods had any number of teachers in his career and changed a teacher at the pinnacle of his career when he won the US Open by 14 shots in 2000. Doug was ready for this commitment challenge. He informed Tom of his decision to engage him and wanted to get started as soon as possible. Tom was pleased with Doug's decision and didn't say much other than, "Let's get started." Doug was elated and ready to commence the next chapter in his life.

The first thing that had to be done was to actually apply

for membership in the California Senior Amateur Golf Association. This is quite a simple process, as the candidate has to commit to play in a number of competitive events. Doug would need a few letters of recommendation attesting to his character and interest in the Association. He would also have to sign off on acknowledging the Code of Ethics in the Association. Fees for membership were nominal, so none of these items presented any issues for Doug, and he would be accepted into the organization by November 1. Membership in the Association is available to all levels of play, irrespective of handicap. The key issue is that the membership has to engage in competitive events, and that involves the time commitment. Doug, with his current handicap of 1.5, would be playing at the highest level and eligible to compete in national USGA (United States Golf Association) championships. Doug sailed through this process, was admitted as a member, and the trek was about to begin.

Competitions involved various formats such as stroke play and match play. There are also two-man and four-man team competitions, as well in stroke play and match play. Doug was fortunate to have his close friend, Brian Kenny, as a mentor to familiarize him with all the various processes of the Association. Brian had retired from his successful career as a small business owner. He had developed a unique set of products for the semiconductor industry and eventually sold his company to the Digital Circuit Corporation for a tidy sum. Brian had just turned 60 and was a +2 handicap player. He had been playing the Senior Amateur for the last nine years and was passionate about the game. Brian was a member of the Rolling Hills Country Club in San Francisco. He'd had a reasonably successful career on the tour, winning a number of tournaments, and was the current Club Champion at Rolling Hills. Doug and Brian had played together for many years, and Brian usually came out on top. He encouraged Doug to join the tour and was elated by Doug's decision. Brian would be a mentor for Doug, as he had plenty of scar tissue from the myriad competitive rounds that he had played and was well aware of the ladder that Doug would have to climb to achieve his objective.

Brian would be a typical player that Doug would be encountering on the Senior Tour. It's important that Doug assesses the level of competition, but must not be intimidated by it. Doug registered for his first tournament: the Stockton City Championship. He started to think about his approach to play in first competitive event on the tour. It would be a two-hour drive from his home in Burlingame for a 9 a.m. registration for the event and to get his starting time. He wasn't happy about the long drive, as he would have to leave the house by 6 a.m. to get there in time to warm up a bit. The Stockton City was a stroke play event, with plenty of good competition expected. Brian was not playing in this event, so Doug would be going to the tournament without knowing anyone.

As Doug started out to Stockton to cross the Dumbarton Bridge, it started to rain. Rain was a possibility in the forecast, and Doug was glad that he had remembered to pack his rain gear and rain gloves. He had never played at the Willow Glen Country Club and was completely unfamiliar with the course. He was a tad apprehensive but optimistic in his swing thoughts and approach to the event. The further he drove toward Stockton, the harder the rain fell, and he started to mentally prepare for a swashbuckling time. He arrived at Willow Glen about 8:30, grabbed a black coffee in the clubhouse, and registered for the event. He would be starting at the 4th hole and proceeded to the driving range to loosen up and shake out the cobwebs from the annoying truck traffic encountered all the way. He warmed up as normal and felt pretty good as he approached the 4th hole tee box to meet his two playing companions. He would be carrying his own bag, to get the experience of focus and making club selections on his own. The horn sounded, and they were off.

Calamity struck quickly. Doug's first tee shot sailed wide right way off the fairway into a thicket of menacing scrub brush. All he could manage with the next shot was a nine iron back into the fairway from the scrub, which was already drenched. He was 240 yards from the green and laced a 3 wood to the 50-yard marker on the par-5 hole. He had some hope that he could up and down from this position and salvage a par on his first hole in a competitive event. His lob wedge flew high and true and had to carry the bunker in the front of the green. The wedge carried the bunker—barely— but backspin from the shot caused the ball to drop into that bunker. The gods of golf had betrayed him, and it felt like a punch in the stomach. His emotions began to rise, and negative thoughts started to creep into his head. He was now in the bunker in four, and his bunker shot was indifferent in the pouring rain. This was not the way to start your round in the first competitive event. Two putts later, a double bogey was already recorded on the card. It was a portent of what was to follow. On his third hole, the par 3 of 200 yards, his five wood was short and found the pond surrounding the green—off to the drop zone where he found the green and 3-putted for a triple bogey. Doug could not recall being 6 over par after 3 holes, ever, and the negative gears in his brain were grinding away. He tried as hard to regroup and silence these negative thoughts. Nothing positive happened on the front nine as he made the turn in 46 strokes—ten over par.

Doug knew that the tournament was essentially over for him, as both his playing partners were both 1 over par. He was embarrassed as he approached the back nine, as his play was poor at best and horrible by his standards. He said to himself, "F…. it" and he decided he had to play the back nine as a practice round. He had to slow things down and concentrate on the good foundation that he had as a player. The strategy worked, as he recorded 3 birdies on the back side, along with 5 bogeys, to shoot a 2 over 38 on the back nine for a round of 84, which placed him near the bottom of the pack. He was dejected but encouraged at the same time. At least he had restored his playing credentials with his playing partners, who came to realize that he could play. They consoled him and congratulated him on his back nine performance. It had rained throughout the round, but he had no excuses. Maybe he had tried too hard, maybe it was the conditions, maybe if this or that happened—there are no maybes, only results that count.

The drive home was even longer and more arduous as he replayed the round over and over throughout the thicket of traffic back to Burlingame. He was determined, as ever, to improve. He started to realize that this quest wasn't going to be easy. He had to relieve himself of self-induced pressure and simply play the game. He walked in the door at 8:30 p.m., pretty exhausted from the experience and the five hours of driving, and broke the news to Becky. Becky was encouraging and positively reinforced the situation. "Look, you shot 38 on the back nine, it's only the beginning so don't worry about it, you'll have plenty of other opportunities—relax and enjoy the experience," she said. "Most golfers couldn't even think about getting to this level, so just go out there and continue," she added. Doug thought about what she said and he had to agree—the glass was still half full. He would get back on the practice range tomorrow with Tom and consider next steps as well as the next event.

Tom was unfazed by Doug's round at Stockton and told him the experience was valuable and had many positives. He had been able to recover the foundation of his game after a terrible front nine and post a two over par on the back nine, which would have placed him in the top quartile of the field. Tom was more impressed with Doug's ability to not give up and stay focused to post this score. Tom began to discuss the concept of consistency in competition. Consistency meant being able to repeat and execute shots routinely. Tom felt that competition adds a bit of adrenalin to the brain, which can cause slight variations in swing tempo and therefore ball impact. The key to dealing with this natural tendency is to realize that it will happen and therefore must be compensated for with focus and deliberation. Most golf fans today have never seen Jack Nicklaus play in his prime. Nicklaus was famous for his intensity and focus; every shot was analyzed intently to the target in a very consistent rhythm. The ability to repeat this tendency time and time again made Nicklaus an intense competitor. Very rarely, if ever, did Nicklaus beat himself; the competitors had to beat him. Tom discussed these concepts with Doug and told him that swing changes were not the answer to improvement in his case. He recommended slight adjustments that would aid in developing consistency and the goal was to eliminate the unforced error. Repetition and developing muscle memory of these adjustments was important through consistent practice. It was also useful to use practice to counteract the influx of adrenalin that would occur every time in competition.

These ideas resonated with Doug as they worked through a number of drills to address the consistency of his swing. Tom used the motto "Practice with a Purpose" to reinforce the concepts that were needed to develop the consistent swing with more predictable results. Doug's putting was also becoming an issue for him, as he struggled during the tournament, but made enough for a respectable 33 putts but that number would have to be reduced to the low thirties or even high twenties if his prospects were going to improve. At this level of competition, putting was often the difference in scoring, since most of these players had excellent ball-striking capability. Doug spent the next two weeks practicing a few hours a day of grooving his swing to a consistent level. The practice sessions really weren't easy and required discipline to hit shots over and over again. It was difficult to avoid becoming defocused and bored since there was no pressure and no adrenalin rush. Nevertheless, Doug persevered and was determined to develop the consistency required. He registered for the Marin Invitational, which would be played in San Rafael, about 15 miles of the Golden Gate Bridge at Woodlands Gap Country Club. Doug was also pleased that Brian would be playing in this event, and the hour drive from home would also add some energy to his game.

The Marin Invitational was set for stroke play on November 20 at the Woodlands Gap Country Club. Doug had played a few rounds there before with some business associates and customers of the bank. Doug felt well prepared for this event. His talks and practice regime with Tom had reinforced his confidence. He left Burlingame with Brian at 7:00 a.m. for the trek over the Golden Gate Bridge to San Rafael. As they crawled through 19th Avenue in the morning traffic, it almost seemed that both men were going to work rather than play in a golf tournament. They didn't discuss the tournament—or golf, for that matter. The day was sunny, bright, and crisp in the Bay Area, a perfect day to play. After a casual warm-up, Doug felt that it was going to be a good day. He teed off on the 471-yard, par-4 first hole and drove it pretty straight, with a bit of fade into the right rough. It was the first cut of rough, so the lie was good and he was able to get a 3 wood on the ball and now had 35 yards left. His chip shot over the right-hand bunker bounced on the green about 6 feet away but rolled away into the greenside rough. Bad break! He chipped the ball to a foot and walked away with an opening bogey. He had played the hole well but didn't get any breaks. He felt that things would improve.

The second hole was a par 3 of 175 yards, and he hit a 6 iron to 3 feet for an easy birdie. He completed the front nine at even par with a number of quality shots, and a little scrambling that netted two birdies and two bogeys. He was even par on the front nine. He really hadn't missed any shots, and if he had a few more putts, he would be under par. Doug now needed to focus on the positive and not become over-confident. The back nine was tougher than the front, so he told himself to take nothing for granted. The 10th and 11th holes were back-to-back terrors. The 10th hole was a 460-yard par 4 where the drive had to clear a hill in the middle of the fairway to have a chance of a medium iron to the green. Doug laced his drive down the middle, and it just crested the hill, so he would have a shot of 195 yards to the green. The fairway sloped severely from right to left, with bunkers ready to catch anything on the left side of the hole. The green also sloped from right to left, similar to the slope of the fairway. Doug decided to draw a hybrid club and hit the ball high to the right, to get the ball to move to the left toward the pin that was on the left. He executed the shot perfectly, as it flew high to the right side of the green, landed, and released toward the hole. It would come to rest about 4 feet from the hole, and he was able to convert the putt for a very good birdie.

The 11th hole was another long par 4 of 485 yards, requiring two well-positioned shots. Doug's tee shot went too far right, with no shot to the green. The hole had a gorge that covered the middle of the fairway and worked its way all the way up to the green, so any shot to the green from the right would be perilous. The best play would be to play defensively and cross the gorge, leaving a pitch shot of 20 yards to try to get up and down. He hit a 5 iron to a spot 30 yards in the front of the green, which sloped severely from front to back. The chip shot had to be below the hole for an uphill putt to make par. He decided to chip the ball past the flagstick to have it roll back toward the pin. It was a risky play, but he executed it to a tap in par. Doug felt that the most difficult part of the golf course was now in the rearview mirror, and he just had to execute his shots—if anything great happened, it would just be gravy on top of a good round. He played the rest of the round flawlessly and came to the house with an even par 72. This score was good enough for 4th place in the event. Brian shot 70 to finish second, so the ride home was a happy one

Thanksgiving and the Christmas holidays were fast approaching, so Doug's thoughts turned to family matters. He would need to plan his schedule for next year's events and set some goals for the year. He felt that he was on the right track, but the schedule would ratchet up in the coming weeks and months. Having focused almost entirely on golf since September, he had to deal with a number of familial responsibilities. He didn't want to lose focus on the progress that he had made in these first two tournaments. He would be hosting the annual Thanksgiving dinner with his children and a number of friends. Doug hated shopping and the whole idea of running out to pick up a Christmas tree and the like. He rejected these things and always played golf with his son and a few friends on Black Friday. This year would be no different, as the tee times were set for a Friday and Saturday outing far from the shopping malls. Becky was pretty tolerant of Doug's tendencies and was more generous than most wives in allowing her husband to pursue his passion. Doug would usually respond, in kind, with an impressive Christmas gift to satisfy Becky's penchant for jewelry. For Doug it was a labor of love, as he had been doing this for over twenty-five years, and she always appreciated it. He would go to the jeweler's on Saturday afternoon in plenty of time to come up with a variety of ideas that could be completed by Christmas Eve. Doug and Becky had two children—a son, Rory, who was twenty-two, and daughter Danielle, twenty. Rory was a senior at Cal Poly Pomona and was a good golfer in his own right. Danielle chose tennis over golf, but her major focus was her budding desire to pursue a writing career at Amherst College in Massachusetts. Doug had not discussed his goals in golf with the children, as it was a private pact between

Becky and him. The children merely thought that Dad was going to pursue something after his brilliant business career, but they didn't know what and were focused on their own personal lives. The holidays would be a quiet time for the Benton family. There would be the obligatory party or two, but the main idea for this holiday season would be to stay around the roost and plan the golf schedule for 2016.

Rory did question his dad about how he was handling retirement or being out of his CEO position. He was interested in Dad's next steps, which pleased Doug, but nothing from him was forthcoming. "Well," he said, "I am still sitting on two public company boards as an independent director. I really haven't decided what I'm going to do down the road, but I'm sure not going to sit around." Rory thought that his parents might do some traveling abroad together, but Doug really didn't volunteer any information. "We'll see," he said. "I've been traveling my entire life, so I'm probably going to want to take a break from that."

Rory played on the Cal Poly Pomona golf team, but he had no aspiration to a career in golf. He enjoyed playing on the team, enjoyed the travel and the competition, but his intention was to graduate from school and pursue a career in investment banking. Although Danielle didn't play golf, she was close to Dad and concerned about his future plans. She also queried him about his plans but received only generalities in reply to her inquiries. She also decided to confide in Mom but didn't get much further with her. Becky knew that Doug wanted to keep this low-key from the family and even friends. The idea was to try to do something special without a lot of fanfare and support, other than Tom—and to a lesser extent, Brian.

The holidays proceeded happily and uneventfully, as Doug and Becky said goodbye to both of the kids, who would return to school on January 3. The holiday season was a welcome respite from the grind of getting his quest off the ground. Doug actually didn't think much about golf during the holidays. It was his first holiday season where he didn't have to host the bank's holiday party and go through the mundane party scene, which he viewed as enforced gaiety. Becky actually felt the same way about these things, but she had been comfortable and effective in the past in playing the role as the boss's wife. She was a gracious hostess, and the Benton Christmas party at their beautiful home was a feature on the local social calendar. Things were toned down this year, which had been planned all along. The party was scrubbed, and the season would be a time for Doug and Becky to spend a holiday season together without responsibilities, so they could relax with each other and their children. It was a smooth season, with entertaining close friends for some intimate dinners, some spontaneous Christmas shopping without asking others to do it, and just hanging out with family and friends. Doug had never been much of a football fan, but he found himself this year watching a number of senseless bowl games to pass the time. They went to a New Year's Eve Party at the home of their close friends, the Ciminos, and Doug now started to get itchy about planning his goals for 2016.

He started thinking about the year, but his mind leapt to the USGA Senior Open, which would be played in August. He then decided on a goal for his golf for 2016—that goal would be to qualify for the US Senior Open. He didn't know if he could achieve such a goal, and it might be a pretty big stretch from where he thought he was in the game, but he decided that would be the goal. He started pondering the potential and probability of such an outcome. He had plenty of excuses as to why it couldn't be done. He didn't have enough experience on the California Amateur Tour—hell, he had played in only two events. He wasn't sure he had the game to play consistently well under pressure. He needed to improve and make swing changes and adjustments to his game, and the question was whether he could implement these changes in time to make a difference and enable the opportunity to achieve the goal. His attitude vacillated between self-doubt and excitement at the same time. He had also decided he had to keep the goal to himself. Some people might argue that this could be viewed as "fear of failure" and not failing in front of peers. Doug was smart enough to realize that nobody really cared about his goal to qualify for the Open Championship. He was just another player on the Tour and someone without a lot of experience. He had been so relaxed during the holiday season that his mind was clear now to figure out how he was going to go about his attempt at the goal.

Doug's emotions vacillated between anxiety and

ambivalence in thinking about his golf game going into the new year. Golf is a terribly mental game. You're never quite sure where you stand in the game, so you have to rely on your foundation to hold ground and try to improve from there. This is very logical idea, but the problem is that the foundation needs practice and focus to be maintained so that improvements can be made.

The big question would be how to prepare a plan for 2016. There were many things to consider. He would have to increase his playing and practice time and continue to work on his weaknesses. Would he continue to work with Tom? Could he maintain his current ball-striking capability? What about the putter? It was his biggest weakness, and he was continuously fiddling with his stroke. At this level of competition, the putter was usually the difference between winning and losing. His mind continued to gyrate between positive and negative thoughts about his game. At this point, Doug was putting a lot of pressure on himself for really no reason. He had to revert to looking at the "big picture"—he had to tell himself not to worry about the game and enjoy the journey no matter how it turned out. He started to think about the process and make certain assumptions, using the precepts that had resulted in a successful business career. Goals are great to have, but the process is more important. It was no different from running the bank. He was completely accountable for the results, so why not just draw on that experience and complete the plan? If the plan required some adjustments, make those adjustments as required. He stopped this grinding process and decided to play in as many tournaments as he could handle and simply—go for it.

He sat down with Becky and related the mental gyrations he was going through. Becky was nonplussed and told him, "Look, you made a decision and you should stick with it. Just give it 100% and never look back and question yourself. We're in this quest together, and I'll support you whatever happens." They had been married for thirty-five years, and Doug quickly came to realize why they had been a good team. He was "stoked" by her support and confidence in him. She realized how important this was to him, as it was going as big a challenge as when he took over as CEO of the bank.

It was pouring rain in the Bay Area as a major winter storm came in, and the Arcadia club had to close the course. There would be no practice time this week, so it was time to gear up mentally for the challenges ahead. He had signed up for the Napa Invitational to be played next week in the wine country. He decided to continue to work with Tom and changed his ideas about his instruction. Tom could help him and recommend, but Doug had the responsibility to execute the details. The Napa event was still a few weeks away, so it was time to ease up a bit on golf. Doug decided to kick back a bit and catch up on some on reading. Doug loved classical literature and he always had a backlog of books that piled up in his study. In past years, he could only read for pleasure on airplanes. He disdained working on airplanes, and he hated reading business books about management and leadership. He didn't think these types of books offered much in the way of advice or assistance in helping him run the bank. He mused a bit about a business book titled *In Search of Excellence*, in which the author chronicled a number of success stories about companies that today were supposed to be the best-managed companies in the world. The fact was that most of these companies were now either out of business, had been acquired by other companies, or simply became irrelevant. Another famous book entitled *Built to Last* was anything but—the covered companies went out of business or couldn't change with the times. He picked up Edith Hamilton's *Mythology* and delved into the world of Greek gods and goddesses. It was a book he had read multiple times over the course of many years from his freshman year in college, and he never tired of the remarkable tales of the Trojan War, Jason and the Argonauts, and the dark verses of Norse and Roman tales. Doug needed this type of release and diversification to keep his mind clear and ready to accept and process new ideas. The rain and wind pelted the windows in his study, as he lay prone on the sumptuous sofa. He hoped that the area would not lose electrical power and ruin the afternoon as he slumped into the travails and inner intrigue of gods and goddesses. After a few hours of magic, he fell fast asleep into a relaxing slumber. The next thing he knew, Becky came in to report that the storm had indeed knocked out the power and they would be dining on salads tonight by candlelight. He would not be able to finish the book tonight but eventually he would get back to it and reabsorb the interesting tales of these creatures.

The next day power was eventually restored as the storm abated in a mizzle of raindrops and fog throughout the Bay Area. He was getting a bit "antsy" to get back to the practice ground, but it was a time to turn to a bit of business. He was a director of a new startup company engaged in the field of artificial intelligence. AI was the latest buzzword in technology, and he had been recently appointed to the board as a potential source for adult supervision of a bright group of technologists from Stanford University. He didn't understand much of the technology, but the assignment provided another source to open his mind to a new experience. He could only provide business acumen and advice for these entrepreneurs. He started to plow through the board materials and noted the lack of strategic content and direction of the company. The technology looked promising, but this company would need a lot of assistance and financing to execute their plans. There was a plethora of technical jargon and acronyms in the materials, which would make for a dysfunctional meeting. He prepared a list of comments and fired them off to the CEO to try to get the meeting back on track. He decided to call Brian to see if he was available for dinner. Brian readily accepted the dinner invitation and they decided to head to Arcadia for an informal night of steak and ale. They discussed the upcoming Napa event and the current state of the games. Each of them predicted the other would win the event, but Doug was clearly more serious about Brian's chances. Brian was a past club champion at Arcadia and was playing well. Brian was encouraged by

Doug's game and he mused, "You're really making progress at this level of competition." They decided to drive up to the tournament together and stay at the Hill Country Inn in downtown Napa the night before the event. The Napa event was an important event for Doug to see if he could maintain the momentum that he felt in his golf swing.

The week before the event, Doug played every day at Arcadia and focused on his putting. He was still working on his alignment and getting the putter back to square. He would place tees on the practice green to drill in the right level of muscle memory to keep the putter on plane with an in to out stroke to avoid missing the short ones. He played five rounds that week with scores in the 70s, but competition would be different, and he had to maintain consistency.

The following Sunday, Doug and Brian headed up to Napa on Sunday afternoon for the Monday event. The sun came up brightly on a brilliant northern California winter morning. It was a chilly 45 degrees. The morning dew and moisture on the grass would eventually give way to a sunny afternoon with temperatures in the high 60s. Doug mused on his good fortune to be in Northern California while the rest of the country faced their wintry weather of snow, ice, and cold. No golf was being played in most, if not all, of the country, and this was one of the few times that he relished being here. There wouldn't be much fairway roll for tee shots on the front nine with the morning conditions, but the course would dry out in the afternoon and play as a completely different venue with faster greens and more generous fairways.

Grapeyard CC was a great course, measuring some 7,100 yards from the back tees, with some terrific holes and challenges. He was encouraged, and he and Brian headed out for some breakfast and on to the practice tee at Grapeyard. Doug loosened up with some stretching and went into his usual practice regime. He was more than prepared and decided to hit a few balls and head for the putting green. It was unusual for him to warm up this quickly—a few pitching wedges and 8 irons. He hit one driver perfectly, and this was it. After a few putts, he proceeded to the first tee to start the round. He didn't pay much attention to his two playing partners other than wishing them well in the event. He crushed his first tee shot right down the middle and fired a 5 iron on the multiple-tiered green and two-putted for a par. The second hole produced a similar result, with a good tee shot and a four iron to the 430-yard par 4. He duck-hooked his drive on the 3rd hole over the bunkers on the left and was fortunate to land in a spot that he had a recovery option. He decided to hit a 4 iron to the 75-yard marker as a shot of 240 yards from his position could have yielded a big number. He hit the 4 iron perfectly to the 75-yard mark. A 56-degree wedge resulted in a putt of 12 feet to make par, and he drained it. His confidence was buoyed by getting through this adversity and was now even after three holes. The par-3 4th hole was 204 yards, and he nailed a 3 iron. The ball sailed onto the green but didn't stick too well, and he ended up 45 feet from the hole—fortunately a two-putt par. The 5th hole was a drivable hole of 300 yards uphill, with a large bunker guarding the front of the green. He decided to play it safe and hit a three wood to the left of the green side bunker and executed the shot perfectly—he got up and down for his first birdie of the day. Another birdie would come on the par-3 7th hole of 180 yards, where he hit a 6 iron to 2 feet for an easy birdie. The 8th hole is a long par 4 of 400 yards with a gigantic ditch guarding the green. His tee shot was true but a bit short, leaving him 180 yards to the hole. He nailed a 5 iron to the middle of that green for another par. The par-5 9th of 576 yards required 3 excellent shots. His tee shot of 250 yards was followed by a 3 wood of 205 yards. The approach shot needed to be right of the pin, since the green had a severe contour from right to left, but his 9 iron was off line and he had 25 feet left for the birdie, which he missed. Nine holes down, and 2 under par so far. Doug took a deep breath and tried to focus on not getting ahead of himself. Things were going well, maybe too well, but he had to block those thoughts out of his mind. His focus thus far was excellent, and he barely took notice of what his playing partners were doing.

He reached into his bag for a banana and headed to the par-3 10th hole of 165 yards. His seven iron was right on line and landed about 8 feet from the cup, but he missed the putt. The next 3 holes were critical to the round. They were long, tough holes, and he had to maintain his concentration. The 11th hole was 467 yards, with severe bunkering from tee to green on the left and trees and bunkers on the right. Doug hit two terrific shots but found himself 20 yards in front of the elevated green—the pitch shot went by the hole by at least 25 feet, and he now faced his first significant challenge to make par. He missed the putt and now stood two under par. The 12th hole was another long par 4 of 445 yards uphill, with water on the left and severe bunkering and rough on the right. Doug's tee shot was a slight miss to the right and wasn't very long. He now faced a shot of some 230 yards uphill to the green, and he pulled a 3 wood. The shot rang out nicely but came to rest in an awkward position 15 yards below the hole just in front of a greenside bunker. The shot required a very delicate pitch, with the goal to be short of the pin for an easier uphill putt. He made great contact with the pitch, but to his dismay, the ball had no backspin and bounded 30 feet past the hole. Another bogey and now two in a row to get him to only one under par. He had to "right the ship" and spanked a 280-yard tee shot on the 535 yard par 5 right down the middle with renewed confidence. It was a very good sign that he could steady the ship and made an easy par.

He came to the par-3 16th hole still at one under par and hit a 6 iron onto the middle of the green for another par. Doug now realized he had a chance to finish pretty high on the leaderboard in this tournament, so the pressure was slightly reduced. He just had to trust what he was doing for the last two holes. After hitting a good tee shot on the par-4 17th hole of 435 yards, he completely missed a 4 iron, flying it right over a bunker and almost carrying it into a ditch. Fortunately, he had a shot of about 90 yards. His 52-degree wedge landed 3 feet from the hole for a wonderful par.

Doug breathed a deep sign of relief as he marched to the 18th tee. The 18th was a par 5 of 560 yards, uphill for the first 280 yards. He smashed his drive to the top of the hill and nailed the next two shots to stare down a putt of 15 feet for birdie. He drained it to finish the round at two under. His third-place finish in the event was completely unexpected but seemed to be a great reward for all the work he had put in on his game over the past four months. He actually bested Brian, who shot a very respectable two over with a ninth-place finish.

The drive home was euphoric, as they both felt like schoolchildren who had just made the honor roll. Of course, they went through the ups and downs of their rounds and were very pleased with their performances in this event. Grapeyard was a good track for both of their games, and they started to plan the next set of events. They started to discuss qualifying for the US Senior Amateur and what it would take to participate in such an event. Doug's entry into the Senior Amateur tour was stimulating and motivating for Brian to improve his game. Brian had tried to qualify for the Senior Amateur on multiple occasions but could never break through. They discussed whether they could both qualify, or help one another so that at least one of them might qualify.

Doug started to think about the impact of his third-place finish. It was completely unexpected, and he started to wonder whether if this was a fluke, or something he could build on. Qualifying for the US Senior Amateur was a pretty audacious goal, but it was starting to come into focus. The question in his mind was whether this performance could be repeated. You can over think these situations, so Doug decided to discard all these thoughts and plan the activities for the coming months of February and March. Becky was euphoric and impressed with this result, and they celebrated the result the next evening at Sam's, their favorite steak house. The dinner completely relaxed Doug as conversation turned to family updates, as Rory was thinking about buying a home in the San Diego area. Next week, he would have to fly to Dallas to attend the other public board that he was on—Cingort Industries. Cingort was a diversified manufacturer of specialty products for the aerospace and defense business, with some exposure to the automotive and telecommunications market. Cingort was a troubled company in need of strategic direction and currently was in the process of refinancing the company. Doug's input and guidance would be very important as Cingort evaluated these strategic objectives. The meeting would be a welcome distraction from golf. Doug felt that he played better when he engaged in other activities, such that golf was a discretionary activity rather than a routine. Going without playing for a few days seemed to increase his focus on his technique, rather than just beating balls. Doug thought about his game and wondered if it would hold up under pressure. Consistency would be the key, with no missed shots during the competitive rounds.

Doug decided to take Becky with him and spend the entire week in Dallas. Becky had some friends in the Dallas area, and the lure of a potential shopping tour was a welcome change in her routine. Perhaps she could wrangle the purchase of another bauble, but that would just be a bonus. He also decided that he wanted to get some practice time, so he made arrangements with Whispering Oaks Country Club through Tom to use the facilities. Doug spent a week before the Dallas trip reviewing Cingort's materials and developing some ideas for the refinancing of the company. CEO Hank Stratton was a bit nervous going into this board meeting, as the company was clearly at a "fork in the road" with respect to its future prospects. CEOs generally bristle at getting "help" or "advice" from independent outside directors, but Hank knew that Doug had the experience to help him, through his extensive banking career. Hank was actually depending on Doug to provide the necessary financing expertise needed for the company to avoid hiring an investment bank.

They stayed at the Ritz Carlton in Dallas, which was close to Cingort's corporate headquarters in downtown. The flight on Virgin Atlantic to Love Field was uneventful. Hank Stratton met them for dinner as they arrived, and he and Doug discussed the plan for the coming week, encompassing a series of financial and operating reviews. Subsequent to these reviews, various scenarios would be created to accommodate the various financing possibilities. Doug would spend the entire week developing these recommendations and wanted to socialize them with the other board members, who would be arriving Wednesday for a board dinner. Committee meetings would commence on Thursday, and the formal board meeting would take all day on Friday.

Doug told Hank he needed some practice time and arranged to play at Whispering Oaks on Wednesday afternoon. Hank had no regard for golf and really didn't understand Doug's passion for the game, but he was in no position to argue with him. Hank would have liked to spend that afternoon with Doug on the plan, but that just wasn't going to happen.

Doug spent the next two days reviewing the company's business in depth. He wasn't sure of what course of action to take, but he had some ideas. On Wednesday afternoon, he headed to Whispering Oaks CC and met Keith Jones, the head professional. Keith was aware of Doug's reputation through his relationship with Tom Smollet at Arcadia. Doug spent two hours going through his bag and still had a few kinks to work out regarding his swing path with the driver and hip position. He spent another hour on chipping and putting. He sat in his hotel room after the session and started to take inventory of his golf skill set:

His current handicap index was 1.8

He had played 78 rounds of golf since November

He had played in eight competitive events with one third-place finish

Could he or should he try to qualify for the US Senior Amateur-USGA Championship?

After some deep thoughts about the rest of his life, he decided to "go for it" and try to qualify. He wasn't getting any younger, and the competition was getting younger. His game plan was to stay within his routine and not over think the game. The goal was to enjoy the journey and see what might happen.

This notion is one of the problems with golf. You tell yourself that you'll try your best and not worry about the results. You try to relieve the pressure on what you are trying to accomplish—fun, good competition—blah, blah, blah. Then you get to the first tee and all of these "mellow feelings" are gone in seconds. All the pressure returns in an instant: the first tee shot has to be good, you have to get off to a good start etc.—it happens to everyone, including the PGA professionals. Doug had played enough competitive golf to recognize all of these feelings, and he would just to have to get on with the task at hand.

Thoughts turned to tomorrow's board meeting. Doug didn't have a lot of confidence in the company's plans. His approach would be deliberate and supportive, but at some point, he would put forth a plan to finance the company. As an independent director, he would have to express his ideas in a way that would look like the plan came from Stratton himself. Doug had no need or desire to control the company, but he wanted to set it on a course for success. The meeting opened casually with the usual pleasantries and legal requirements. The company needed to raise money for its new product initiatives, as the company's free cash inflows were insufficient to finance the expansion from operations. The company's balance sheet was in decent shape, so debt capacity could be added, but the question was whether to raise the funds from a short-term revolving credit arrangement or borrow on a longer fixed- rate debt obligation. The long-term model would be advantageous if the company's future cash flows were predictable, to cover the servicing of the debt with principal and interest payments. The short-term revolving credit arrangement would provide interest rates that would fluctuate and be susceptible to volatility depending on economic conditions. Doug covered this thoroughly with Hank and came to the conclusion that long-term debt was the preferable option, for these reasons.

It was predictable as to how much principal and interest payments were required, and this could be evaluated against the company's ability to generate free cash flow to service the obligations. The directors, including Doug and Hank, were convinced that the company's business was strong to handle this type of obligation. The decision was made to "go long," and the process turned out to be very collaborative by the board. Hank was very pleased, as a significant strategic matter that had troubled him for quite some time had been resolved.

Doug and Becky headed back to San Francisco in a good frame of mind, as Doug had helped resolve a thorny problem. Becky found a diamond pendant to her liking and Doug shrugged it off, as he was pleased with the entire trip.

The following Saturday was the beginning of Arcadia's Match Play Championship. Conditions were good in Northern California, as sunny weather with temperatures in the high 60s were becoming the norm in this time of year. The greens were pretty fast and registered almost 12 on the stimp meter. Doug qualified for the Championship Flight on Saturday with a smooth 75. The Championship Flight was set and play commencing on Sunday. Doug would be giving opponents 1-2 strokes a side in these early matches. The first match was against Dennis Weaver, a 36-year-old private wealth manager with a 5 handicap, so Doug would be giving him three shots for this round. It was a close match throughout the day as Dennis took a 1 Up lead into the turn. After 17 holes, the match was All Square and it looked like the match might needed to be settled in extra holes. On the 410-yard, par 4, Dennis was on the green in two, with a 25-foot attempt for birdie. Doug was in the front bunker, with the prospect of having to get up and down to take the match to extra holes. Doug proceeded to hole the bunker shot in front of Dennis' birdie putt for a birdie 3. Dennis couldn't convert the 25 footer and Doug won the match-1 UP. As I said many times before, never underestimate what your opponent can do in a match plan situation. The following Saturday, the next match was against former club champion Art Howe, but this was not Art's day. Doug thrashed him 6 and 5 to move to the final match on Sunday. Ken Mercer emerged from the alternate bracket. Ken was playing very well, and Doug had to give him three shots. Ken holed an 8 iron on the 11th from 145 yards for an eagle 2 to even the match. On the 16th hole with Doug 2 down, Ken hit a terrible drive down the left side of the fairway, leaving him 225 yards on the 390-yard par 4. Ken had to cross the creek and avoid the 3 greenside bunkers guarding this treacherous hole. Ken nonchalantly took his driver out of his bag, to his caddie's amazement, and knocked it onto the green and into the hole for another eagle 2—end of match and the end of the competition for Doug. Doug congratulated Ken on his impressive 3 and 2 victory, but Doug felt pretty good about his state of his game—not too many people could do what Ken had done. Doug was playing well, and his swing was holding up under pressure—he didn't lose this. Even Ken Mercer excelled with stellar play and was 3 under for the entire match at Arcadia.

Doug went back to his decision regarding the US Senior Amateur. He would have to qualify in a number of events to get into the national tournament. First local qualifying, regional qualification, and then he must continue to win, to proceed to the best 32 senior amateurs in the country. Stroke plan would eliminate one-half of the field to 16 players. The top 16 players would then compete in match play until a champion emerged.

Doug called Brian and asked if he was going to give it another try. Brian had tried for four years to make to the final field of 36 but never got past local qualifying. Brian had some confidence in the current state of his game and stated that he was going to give it another shot. Doug was excited at the prospect of trying to make it with Brian. They started to discuss practice regimen and some other competitive events prior to the qualification events.

The Senior Amateur is a United States Golf Association Championship and has been played for the last 65 years.

There are about 2400 participants who can compete in the event, provided their handicap index is 7.4 or less. The average age of the participant is 60. Qualifying rounds begin in mid July leading up to the final matches during the last week of August. Qualifying sites are in all 50 states. Applications were due by the end of April and qualifying site play would begin in the mid-July time frame.

Doug and Brian decided to mark their decision with a best ball match against each other on Saturday at Arcadia to get their juices flowing. Neither of them played very well, and Brian won the match on the last hole by sinking a 15-foot putt for par. Doug pressed a ten-dollar bill into Brian's hand for the value of the victory. They didn't break 80 and they were unimpressed with their performance but enjoyed the day anyway. Doug headed home to grab a quiet dinner with Becky. It had been a busy month and there were busier times ahead, but for now, it was time to relax.

It was now mid-March, and the rainy season in northern California would be ending soon. Doug went about getting the paperwork from the United States Golf Association to get his entry in. He took a quick look on the USGA site to see the qualifying sites that he would be playing in. He assumed that he would be playing in either the northern California or central California qualifying site. The application wasn't due until the beginning of July, but he would have to submit a Performance Form to the USGA. The Performance Form is a requirement of the USGA that substantiates that the individual has the eligible handicap index and that performance in competitive tournaments would have to be verified by a third party. The USGA would either approve or disapprove the application on the basis of this process. Doug had played enough competitive rounds in the past two years to get approved for inclusion into the qualifying field. The grand total of qualifiers throughout the United States would eventually be whittled down to 64 players. The top gross scores from the qualifying sites would eventually play off until the top 64 players were determined. The final 64 players would then proceed to the Championship Tournament Site for six rounds of knockout match play that would eventually determine the USGA Senior Amateur Champion.

The weeks went quickly as the rainy season in northern California, and it probably wouldn't rain again until October. Doug stepped up his practice time and consulted with Tom to work on a number of different things to achieve the consistency that would be needed in upcoming events. The next two months would be spent in a number of competitive events throughout the Bay Area and Northern California. Doug continued to play a number of competitive matches with Brian as they both went about their business to prepare for the qualifying events for the US Senior Amateur. Doug started to realize what the professionals on the PGA Tour have to do in hitting a number of balls per day and working on little things in their swing to achieve the required consistency to maintain a living as a touring professional. Doug had none of these financial concerns, but qualifying for the amateur was something he believed he was ready and poised to accomplish. He had reached the pinnacle of the business world, and he wanted to prove that his golf capability to achieve his objective of qualifying for the final 64 players. Doug cleared his calendar and was able to escape most of his business obligations for the next few months. The social calendar was scrubbed; Becky would throw some small parties for friends as summer approached, but nothing too lavish that might distract Doug from his endeavors.

The first qualifying site was at Beaver Creek Country Club in Lafayette over in the East Bay, about 45 miles from home. Beaver Creek was the northern California qualifying site. Doug received his acceptance letter at the end of May and the first round of qualifying would be played in the second week of July. As the time approached, Doug started to vacillate his feelings within a wide range of enthusiasm to despair. He continually had to fight the negative feelings that form the mental part of the game. At this level, the mental part of the game is equally and perhaps more important than the physical part of the game. You must have the execution skills mentally to be able to dial up the physical skills to score. Just last week, Doug was on the 18th hole in a tournament in San Francisco and had hit an indifferent tee shot that was rather short but in the fairway. He nailed a 3 wood for his second but still had a third shot of 188 yards uphill to the green on this 596-yard par 5 with huge bunkers on either side of green. To the dismay of his caddie, he pulled a 2 wood out of his bag, which he hardly ever hit. He needed distance and height to carry the ball back to the pin, and his caddy was skeptical and called for a 3 iron. Doug decided to hit the 2 wood and nailed it to 15 feet of the hole and made the left to right slider for a birdie and a 1UP victory in his match. In thinking about this shot, Doug was absolutely convinced that he could execute the shot, and he was proven right. His caddy would have bet a thousand to one against him and Doug would have lost the match.

The next few months of May and June went by pretty quickly, as Doug played in a number of events at the club or at nearby clubs. He continued to take lessons from Tom, but you really couldn't call them lessons. Tom was taking more of the role of mentor, golf confidant, cheerleader, etc. to reinforce Doug's capabilities. Tom felt that, despite all the hard work, it would still be difficult for Doug to reach the finalist round. Tom liked many aspects of Doug's game, but he was concerned that all the concentrated effort that Doug put forth in the last six months would not be sufficient to overcome the mental aspects of the game. Players at this level had been trying for years to make the final qualifying round and had the battle scars brought on by experience. You often see the same phenomenon on the PGA Tour. A young player who has never won on tour plays three spectacular rounds and leads a PGA event through 54 holes. More often than not, the young professional succumbs to the pressure of winning his first PGA event having to play the final round in the final group. The failing young professional usually takes away a lot of learning from the final-round collapse and eventually breaks through. Sometimes this happens more than once to the professional player.

Brian Kenny was a good example of a fine player who was unable to get over the hump to get to the final 36. Brian had a lot of "scar tissue" (missed opportunities) over the last six years that he had tried to qualify. Brian was pleased that Doug was making this attempt, and it was motivating for him; he was thinking at age 60, this could be his last shot at it. They played in each other's member guest tournaments at Arcadia and Rolling Hills. Those events drew some very good competition in the First Flight of the event and they played well enough to win the pari-mutuel betting and the horse race at the Arcadia event. Momentum was building for the first round of the qualifying round at the Beaver Creek.

It was July 20, and the first round of the Senior Amateur Tour Qualifying round for the USGA Championship. Over 2400 contestants with a certified handicap of 7.4 or less would be teeing it up nationwide for about 200 slots that would eventually narrow to 64 participants for the national championship. Doug and Brian decided to practice on Sunday afternoon and stay at the Lafayette Park Hotel that evening to forego the murderous commute from Burlingame that would occur the following morning. Beaver Creek Country Club was only 45 miles from Doug's home, but the Bay Area had become a traffic nightmare and that trip on a Monday morning would take over 90 minutes to get to the course. Fighting traffic to get to the course on a Monday morning to make an 8 a.m. tee time would not be a good way to start this challenge. Beaver Creek was well suited to Doug's game and had a lot of similar features to Arcadia, so he seemed to be in his comfort zone. Beaver Creek would measure out at 7,250 yards from the tees being utilized for the qualifier. Doug and Brian had spent months preparing for this event, and now was the time to execute. Doug and Brian survived this qualification, as each of them shot 72 to finish in the top 3 qualifiers for the next qualifying round. Doug had a roller coaster round and got off to a poor start, pulling his tee shot on the first hole into the left rough. He was lucky to make bogey as he scrambled around this hole and drained a 15-foot putt for bogey. It was not the way he thought things would start, and he was upset with himself.

Things didn't get any better, and after five holes, he was four over par, but a sense of calm entered the picture. Many players would cave in to this situation, but Doug regrouped and stabilized his game, hitting tee shots in the fairways and finding greens in regulation. At the ninth hole, he still hadn't made a birdie and was still four over par. His second shot on the 424-yard par 4 found the greenside bunker with a good lie. Doug holed the bunker shot for a birdie 3, and this shot changed his demeanor and approach to the rest of the round. He seemed to cross over into another mental zone as the game became almost easy and routine. He birdied the next three holes to get back to even par with four birdies in a row. His putter was ablaze, and the holes looked as big as garbage cans. Beaver Creek was well known for its tough finishing holes, but Doug kept executing his shots consistently. He found little trouble in the final six holes, but no birdies were forthcoming, so he finished at even par 72. He had no idea if this would be good enough to qualify, but it was, and he was pretty excited. Brian also qualified with a round of 72 that was achieved in quite a different way, with a 32 on the front nine, and he had some pressure on him to make par on the closing hole to complete an even round 72. He made a 20-foot putt for par on the 18th and rapped his chest a few times, as this putt was needed to get to the next round.

The drive back to Burlingame was pretty ecstatic, as both Doug and Brian replayed their rounds with each other. Becky was waiting with champagne to celebrate their initial success. Their games had held up under the pressure, and their confidence level was high. Doug knew from some past experience not to get too excited about their chances. Golf was a game where you could go from champ to chump and not even know why or how it happened. He mused that golf was a mystery with almost an infinite number of variables. He tried to think of an analogy, but nothing really fit—you just had to play as well as you could with those variables, and keep them in a range that could produce success. Brian was wondering what happened to him on the back nine at Beaver Creek after a blistering front nine. He couldn't understand where his swing went slightly awry to produce a 4 over back nine and having to make a 20-footer to win his place. After some discussion, Doug told him, "Forget about the back nine, and think about how you produced the great score on the front side. It's always terrific to get off to a good start and build momentum, and that's what you accomplished today."

In two weeks, they would get the chance they were aiming for. The national field would be cut to the final 64 to play for the championship. The top 64 gross scores would be the measure to get to the final match plan competition. There were about 250 players left to compete for the final rounds, and undoubtedly there would be a number of ties, requiring extra holes for the final spots. The qualifying site for California would be Sea Cliffs Country Club in San Diego. Sea Cliffs was an interesting mix of some wide-open holes by the ocean, and narrower tree-lined inland holes. It reminded Doug of Spyglass Hill at Pebble Beach, albeit a bit easier. Doug had the feeling he was playing with "house money." While he hoped he might get this far, the probability was pretty low, and he was testing the odds of the golf gods. His performance thus far reminded him of a PGA Tour professional trying to win his first professional event. The professional had won many amateur events and pro mini tour events, so he had the experience of the winner's circle. But winning a PGA Tour event was another pinnacle that he had to be reached with some sacrifice, and usually the professional loses after leading the tournament or being a position to win, as the pressure is at a higher level. Doug felt the same way but tried to rationalize his situation by thinking this was a level of pressure that he should not feel. Nevertheless, he was feeling it. Competing for the USGA Senior Amateur Championship would be the fulfillment of a lifelong achievement in golf. It is a state of "rarified air" for the amateur golfer. Brian had never gotten this far in all his years of trying, so he felt that he had already accomplished a personal best that would be undeniable.

The stage was set as Doug and Brian booked their Southwest Airlines flight to San Diego. This time Doug would have a gallery. Rory was going to caddie for him and Becky and Danielle were flying down as well to witness the proceedings. Doug was euphoric that Rory was "on the bag," and this was an experience that they would never forget. After the quick 90-minute flight to San Diego, the group checked into the hotel while Doug and Rory made plans to play a practice round at Sea Cliffs. Tom Smollet had made all the arrangements and would fly down himself on Monday to give Doug some final instructions and tips for the round he was about to play. The final qualifier would be held on Wednesday. Doug was really pleased to have the whole family, as the kids had to take some unscheduled vacation time, but they wanted to watch their dad try to realize his dream. Becky and Danielle scheduled some spa appointments for Monday, while Doug and Rory would spend Monday charting Sea Cliffs and meeting with Tom. Doug really liked Sea Cliffs. He had never played it before, but it was course that was suitable to his eye. The opening holes meandered towards the ocean with some spectacular views. The course then moved inward, shaped by oak trees. The rough was set up to be a bit penal but not impossible. The greens were very quickly and probably were at a level 12 or 13 on the stimp meter, which is very close to PGA Tour standard. On Monday night, Doug hosted a dinner for the family with Brian and Tom at the hotel. The topic of the impending event was avoided, as conversation turned into a review of the spa facilities and the shopping trip that Becky had with Danielle. Doug would have a conference call with one of the public boards on Tuesday and then head back out to Sea Cliffs just to hit some balls and spend some time on the practice putting green.

Wednesday came, and Rory dutifully prepared his chart book and inventory of Doug's bag for the day ahead. It was a bright, beautiful, sunny day in San Diego with just a hint of wind, which would potentially bode well for scoring. Doug had an 8:12 tee time, and they were on the range by 6:45. Doug felt very good about the swing that he brought to the course today and hoped he could maintain this rhythm on the golf course. After ten minutes on the practice putting green, Doug set off for his tee time and stopped to wish Brian luck. Deep down, he was hoping that one if not both could play well and get through this level of qualifying to reach the final 64. Doug laced his first tee ball right down the middle of the par-5 1st hole. His second shot was a 2-iron hit at 230 yards, which left him only a chip shot of some 25 yards to hit the ball. He didn't execute the chip shot very well and he came up 25 feet short of the hole, so he two-putted for a disappointing par. The front nine would continue in this vein with good tee shots followed up with indifferent iron shots or poor chip shots, but he was still even par through 9.

In prior competitive events, Doug might have lost his emotional stability and focus and lost shots to par. Today he was grinding and suppressed these emotions and took what the golf course gave him. Things would get worse for Doug before they would get better. He bogeyed the par-5 10th hole, which was actually a good bogey, as the second shot found the water in front of the green. He was able to land a chip shot from the landing area to about two feet for the bogey. On the next hole, he pull- hooked a 6 iron into the trees on the left of the par 3 hole and recorded another bogey. He had to pull it together and do it quickly, as he was running out of holes. He felt that even par or better would be needed to qualify for the finals, and it was time to pull it together. Things looked dire as he pushed his tee shot to the right on the par-4, 422-yard 12th hole, but a fortuitous bounce off the tree placed the ball back in the fairway some 190 yards away. Doug selected a 4 iron for the approach shot, and Rory interceded and suggested a 5 iron. Rory felt that Dad just had a little too much adrenaline, so best to hit the club that would not risk going through the green, which would present a very difficult shot to make par. Reluctantly Doug agreed, and it turned out to be a good decision. The 5 iron flew straight and true and landed 3 feet from the hole. Doug gave Rory a high five as they strolled off the 12th hole. A fortuitous ricochet off an oak tree had presented Doug with perhaps the greatest stroke of luck in his amateur career.

Doug birdied the next two holes and now stood one under par as he approached the 16th tee. He made routine pars on the next two holes and found himself in the greenside bunker on the 18th hole. On this hole, he and Rory didn't agree on club selection, and Doug clanked a 7 iron as Rory wanted him to step on an 8 iron. The lie in the bunker wasn't great. It was a bit downhill, and a bunker shot like this would be difficult to stop as it approached the hole. Doug opened the club face as wide as possible. He would have to hit down on the sand from this lie to propel the ball out of the bunker and hopefully get it to close enough so he could make par. He took a three-quarter swing back, and the ball went swirling out of sand toward the ball with a bit too much speed and then the improbable happened—thwack!—the ball hit the flagstick hard, but in the right place, and dropped right into the hole for an improbable birdie. Doug had a three under par 69, and now he would have to wait to see if this was good enough to qualify for the Finals. His round was one of the earlier ones, and a number of groups were to follow. Scoring conditions for Sea Cliff were very good on this day, and with the skill level of these players, Doug wasn't sure that his 69 would be good enough, but it turned out that it was. The Benton family was ecstatic. Doug combed the leader board for Brian and was encouraged to see that Brian was 2 under par through 15. He would complete his round with a 2 under 70 and qualify by one stroke. They were both headed to Ohio for the final matches in two weeks.

The scene was now set for the final matches that would determine the USGA Senior Amateur Championship at Armstrong National Golf Club just outside Columbus, Ohio. Doug was so pleased that he couldn't quite believe it. He was on a roll and had never played this well in his life.

He had to toss those thoughts out of his mind and think of what was ahead. From here on in, he would be competing in a match play format and would have to win 5 matches to win the championship. He knew he had to take it one hole at a time, one match at a time to just stay in contention and keep playing. The goal was simple—play well enough to keep playing. It was useless trying to plan for these matches. You simply had to hope that you could continue to execute in the way that got you to this spot. The additional challenge was that not only did you have to play well, but you had to play well enough to beat your opponent. At this level, anyone could beat anyone on any given day. The matches would begin on August 4, so Doug and Brian began making their preparations for the trip to Ohio with their respective families. Neither of them had ever played at Armstrong National, so they wanted to get there early to get a couple of practice rounds in. Tom Smollett was pretty excited for Doug's success and decided to make the trip as well. Doug really appreciated Tom's participation, as his presence gave him the opportunity to take a close look at his mechanics as he prepared for his match. This was a knock-out competition—lose and go home.

Doug was pretty amazed that he had made it to the Finals. It was pretty unlikely, particularly with the limited experience he had at this level of competition. Now, it really didn't matter—he was here at the Finals, and he would do the best he could in the circumstances. He had no idea if he could continue this level of play. He just had to trust his swing mechanics and see how far it might take him.

His first opponent was Matt Zeinke from Davenport, Iowa. Zeinke was Club Champion of Sycamore Country Club in Davenport, which was in southeastern Iowa, pretty close to the Illinois border. Doug and Matt exchanged pleasantries and teed out at 7:47 a.m. on Armstrong. Doug had a few concerns on his swing path on the driving range and was thinking about making a few adjustments. Tom advised him against making any changes and told him to visualize the results he had been getting on his march to the Finals. Doug striped the drive right down the middle about 265 yards, and Matt whizzed one by him at the 290-yard mark. They both made par and the game was on. It seemed to Doug that Matt was the better player, but he had to ignore and suppress that thought. At this skill level, anyone could be beaten on any given day. Matt birdied the 4th hole to go one up, as his 165-yard iron shot ended up five feet below the hole, which he converted for the first birdie of the day. Doug responded with another terrific up and down from the green side bunker on number 9 to halve the match. Both of them were one under through the turn. Matt had significantly more experience in this championship, having reached the quarter-finals twice in prior years. The match now would come down to the last nine holes.

Doug seemed to be in a zone he had never experienced. He was playing on complete instinct, without paying much attention to what Matt was doing. They were both making pars and birdies and playing pretty flawlessly. Doug's big break came on the par-5, 572-yard hole when his 6 iron from 160 yards for his third shot landed 10 feet from the hole and stopped there. Matt only had 127 yards to the hole and he flipped a pitching wedge towards the hole, which spun backwards nearly off the green from the lower pin position. He needed to hole a 25-foot putt for his birdie, and to put significant pressure on Doug, but his putt lipped out to the left. Doug now had a 10-foot putt up the hill to close out the match, and he drained it to win the match 1UP. It was a remarkable and improbable victory for Doug and a tough loss for Matt, as both contestants played well enough to have beaten anyone in the field today. Doug had beaten a player with significantly more experience and who had already experienced the pressure of this event.

The magic for Doug continued, as he won his next four matches against very worthy opponents. It seemed that Doug was the Cinderella story of this event, as he now found himself in the final championship match against a most unlikely opponent. Brian had survived some sloppy play with a barrage of birdies at just the right time to win all of his matches against formidable opponents. The situation was completely imponderable. Doug was going to play his mentor, Brian Kenny, for the USGA Championship. What a remarkable turn of events. Just six weeks ago, they had played a match together at Arcadia for fun, and both of them didn't even break 80. Now they were about to play for the USGA Senior Amateur Championship. It would be an All Northern California Final. Doug was very pleased and intrigued at the same time. Both of them had played so many rounds together, and Brian was clearly the more experienced and better player. Brian had won most of the time they played together and there was a time when Brian would be giving Doug two strokes a side. The question for Doug was whether this pairing would be an advantage or a disadvantage in a pressure-packed Championship Final in Columbus, Ohio. Doug felt that he would really have to focus on playing as well as he could, without worrying what Brian might do in this situation. They decided to have dinner together the night before the match with the families to relieve the pressure that tomorrow would certainly bring.

Championship Saturday arrived at Armstrong CC and the sun was shining brightly with little wind and no rain in the forecast for a brilliant August day. Both Doug and Brian warmed up on the range together and decided to have a $100 bet on their match. I'm sure that this was a first for a national championship with two close friends competing for a national championship as if it were a normal Saturday afternoon. They weren't sure if the bet would be within USGA rules, so they decided that collection of the bet wouldn't be disclosed or satisfied until they were back in northern California. The competition would be 18-hole match play and they promptly teed off at 10 a.m.

Doug whacked his first tee shot in the left rough and would have difficulty making par from that position, as his ability to navigate around a bunch of trees was unsuccessful. Brian striped his drive about 280 yards and easily made par to take an immediately 1UP lead. Doug was not happy and grimaced as his 16-foot par ran by the hole. On to Number 2—Brian had the honor and laced another spectacular drive down the fairway about 280 yards. Doug pulled himself together and found himself just in the left rough with a lie that looked like a flier. With 142 yards to go, Doug selected a 9 iron to account for the lie and hoisted the ball high in the air, which settled about 7 feet from the hole. Brian's pitching wedge from 120 was just inside Doug. Doug felt that he had to make this putt, in order to generate some momentum and put some pressure on Brian. Putts at Armstrong seemed to be breaking right at the hole all week, and they had not experienced this pin position. Doug read the putt to break a ball out to the right, and now he had to make the putter blade execute his command. The putt broke as he read and snaked in the hole for a birdie. Brian surveyed his putt from all sides, but he couldn't convert, as the ball hung on the lip of the cup but wouldn't go in. The match was now All Square.

Doug had to fight the urge of focusing on Brian instead of his game. They had been friendly competitors for a long time, and Doug would have never have thought that he would be in this position, let alone be competing against a good friend for a national championship. Brian seemed oblivious to the circumstances, and it seemed to Doug that he was very focused. There wasn't a lot of conversation as they headed for the 3rd tee. The 3rd hole was a long one of 215 yards, with a pond surrounding the left side of the hole. Brian still had the honor and selected a 4 iron and was able to find the front part of the green. It was an aggressive play, but it resulted in an uphill birdie opportunity of 25 feet. Doug selected a hybrid club and just caught the edge of the green avoiding the water by a "smidge" as the ball faded in as he had hoped it would do. He still had a 45-foot putt that would break about 8 feet from right to left. He had to get this one close since Brian had a much better opportunity for birdie. Doug's approach putt was too high and too fast, and he now had a 10- footer back up the hill for his par. Brian two-putted easily for a par. Doug missed the 10-footer for a bogey, as he misjudged the speed and came up just short. Brian had a 1UP lead.

Doug started to think about the grind of this match. It seemed they were matching shot for shot, and there was little margin for error. Doug took a deep breath and tried to refocus his efforts at the task at hand. There would be no room for error today, or inconsistency. If he was going to win, he was going to have to refocus and play the course shot by shot and not be concerned about Brian or the potential outcome or even what was at stake. This is extremely hard to do, but Doug felt it was probably a once-in-a lifetime opportunity.

The match continued to be nip and tuck as Doug managed a birdie on the par 4, 392- yard 7th hole, and Brian made another birdie on the par-3, 166-yard, 9th hole where he holed a bunker shot for a birdie. Doug experienced the pain of match play as he had knocked his 6 iron to 11 feet but converted the putt as he watched Brian slam his bunker shot into the hole for a birdie 2. Nine holes to go, and Brian was 1UP.

They both bogeyed the very difficult 462-yard, par-4 11th as both guys managed to knock their 3 wood approach shots in the gorge on the right. The wind had come up to push both shots a lot further than either player intended. The pressure was mounting on both of them as Brian maintained a 1UP lead, but that was the largest lead in the match. It was getting pretty exciting as they headed for the clubhouse. It was just about 12:30 and the wind started to blow pretty hard against the players—it was at least a one-club and maybe even a two-club wind. Doug needed a birdie on the 18th hole to halve the match as Brian maintained his 1UP lead throughout the back nine. He was calm, and he approached the 18th tee. He had played his heart out and grinded all the way. He never thought he would be in this position, and he recounted in his head all that he accomplished these past months. These thoughts were not stimulating but almost soothing. He ripped his best tee shot of the day right down the middle about 280 yards on the par-5, 552-yard hole. He actually no longer cared what Brian was doing, as he decided his fate would be in the hands of the golfing gods.

Doug decided not to go for the green in two, as he felt it was a low-percentage shot. The goal was to get the ball within 75 yards and leave it to his short game to get the birdie. Heck, Brian might make birdie as well, so no reason to throw it away now on a low-percentage shot. Doug played his 3 wood well and smashed the ball to the 65- yard mark. Brian laid up also to about 50 yards. Doug drew his trusted gap wedge. It was one of the best clubs in his bag, so now was the time to execute the chip shot of his life. The wedge ran high and true and almost went into the hole—and stopped about a foot away. The gallery was ecstatic with this shot, and this would certainly be a conceded birdie. Brian had a similar shot with his sand wedge, but the ball took a weird hop without a lot of backspin and settled some 17 feet away. It was going to come down to this final putt. Speed was going to be important, and the putt was a double breaker right to left and left to right at the hole—certainly not an easy one. Doug just looked on and was ready to accept whatever happened. The smallish gallery was tense and pensive as Brian read the putt, released the putter blade, and MISSED! It lipped the cup and went sliding a foot from the hole. Doug conceded the putt with an act of friendship and good sportsmanship—it was a good call on his part. THE MATCH ENDED ALL SQUARE AND A PLAYOFF WOULD COMMENCE IMMEDIATELY.

After a few gasps, handshakes, hugs, and the like, everyone composed themselves and the USGA officials congratulated both players. It certainly had been an exciting match, full of drama and intensity—an unlikely event for two friends to be competing for a national championship. After a brief break and the signing of scorecards, etc., they proceeded again to the 18th tee to start the sudden-death playoff. The first player to win a hole would be the USGA Senior Amateur Champion golfer of the year. They picked two golf balls out of a pot, with one ball with a dot and one without. The player that picked the ball without a dot would have the honor of going first. There is a lot of conjecture about whether there is an advantage to going first, and most people would say it is an advantage, as your opponent has to match or better what you do. Doug picked the ball without a dot and was up on the tee. The adrenaline was really flowing, and Doug could hardly feel his body. His mechanics were on remote control as he smashed his tee shot down the middle of the fairway one more time on this hole. Brian did the same and almost ended in the same place, where he was 30 minutes only a bit farther back at the 60-yard marker.

Doug took out his 3 wood again and really pummeled it this time. It was almost as if he were going for the green as the ball ran past Brian to the 40-yard mark. It looked like both gentlemen would make birdie, and the match would then proceed to the 15th hole. Brian grabbed that sand wedge and this time put a little extra "mustard" on the shot and it spun back to where Doug's ball had settled in regulation play—a conceded birdie, for sure. Doug now had to stare down this short pitch shot and at least get close enough to convert a birdie to keep the match going. This time, Doug grabbed his 56-degree sand wedge and surveyed the shot. He took the club back deliberately and swept it cleanly toward the hole. What happened next was incredible. The ball hit the flag itself on the flagstick and dropped into the hole for an EAGLE 3! Match over—Doug was the national champion. What a way to finish a championship match—Brian could only manage a wry smile and remember—never underestimate what your opponent will do in match play.

Doug's odyssey ended in dramatic fashion. He couldn't believe that he had come this far and had achieved his objective, which was a distant dream about ten months ago. His victory could be viewed as "lucky" by all the competitors that had been trying to get to this position for years, but golfers don't tend to think that way. They congratulate those with skill and good fortune, while they continue to hone their own game for additional attempts at the prize.

CPSIA information can be obtained
at www.ICGtesting.com
Printed in the USA
FSHW021725180419